DAIRY

MADE Easy

FOOD STYLIST **AMIT FARBER**

PHOTOGRAPHY **DANIEL LAILAH**

ASSISTANT STYLIST **RENEE MULLER**

DESIGN **RACHELADLERDESIGN.COM**

PUBLISHER **MESORAH PUBLICATIONS, LTD.**

Leah Schapira & Victoria Dwek

D1403866

© Copyright 2014 by **Mesorah Publications, Ltd.**

First Edition — First Impression / May 2014

ALL RIGHTS RESERVED

No part of this book may be reproduced in any form, photocopy, electronic media,
or otherwise — even for personal, study group, or classroom use — without written
permission from the copyright holder, except by a reviewer who wishes to quote brief
passages in connection with a review written for inclusion in magazines or newspapers.

THE RIGHTS OF THE COPYRIGHT HOLDER WILL BE STRICTLY ENFORCED.

Published by **ARTSCROLL / SHAAR PRESS**
4401 Second Avenue / Brooklyn, NY 11232 / (718) 921-9000
www.artscroll.com

Distributed in Israel by **SIFRIATI / A. GITLER**
Moshav Magshimim / Israel

Distributed in Europe by **LEHMANNS**
Unit E, Viking Business Park, Rolling Mill Road
Jarrow, Tyne and Wear, NE32 3DP / England

Distributed in Australia and New Zealand by **GOLDS WORLD OF JUDAICA**
3-13 William Street / Balaclava, Melbourne 3183, Victoria / Australia

Distributed in South Africa by **KOLLEL BOOKSHOP**
Northfield Centre / 17 Northfield Avenue / Glenhazel 2192 / Johannesburg, South Africa

ISBN-10: 1-4226-1488-3 / ISBN-13: 978-1-4226-1488-4

Printed in Canada by Noble Book Press

ACKNOWLEDGMENTS

We ALWAYS SAY THAT OUR IDEAS AREN'T OURS.

We can be totally stumped, but then **Hashem** inserts something brilliant into our heads. We owe Him credit for every little teaspoon in this book.

Thank you to our chief taste testers, our **husbands** and **children**, our encouraging parents, and the rest of our family. You helped cook, taste, babysit, and give valuable feedback. Thanks especially for your patience during the weeks of photo shoots. We hope you were buttered up (literally!) with the selection of pizza, pasta, and those heavenly dairy desserts.

After the recipes were completed and tested, it takes the brilliance of our creative team to turn them into the book you see: our stylist, **Amit Farber**, our photographer, **Daniel Lailah**, our graphic artist **Rachel Adler**, and operations manager **Zalman Roth**.

Thank you to our assistant stylist, the talented **Renee Muller**. You're not just one of our colleagues, we value your friendship as well. Thank you to **Set Your Table**, your dishes always help make our books beautiful; **Chaya Sarah Thau**, for supplying some of the amazing tablecloths you see in the photos; and to **Esti Waldman** for coming through at the last minute.

The **ArtScroll** team's dedication and enthusiasm is invigorating. Thanks to **Rabbi Meir Zlotowitz**, **Gedaliah Zlotowitz**, editor **Felice Eisner**, designers **Eli Kroen** and **Devorah Bloch**, PR Manager **Miriam Pascal**, proofreaders **Judi Dick** and **Tova Ovits**, and to the rest of the staff who kept things moving.

Thank You!

Leah and Victoria

Thanks to the cookkosher members who keep on stimulating us with their ideas.

Whenever we were inspired by a cookkosher member's contribution, you'll find the member's name next to the recipe. In appreciation, they'll each be receiving a copy of this cookbook.

We hope you enjoy these delicious, tried and true recipes, and that they encourage you to have fun creating delicious meals for your families. And we hope we've made it easy, too.

ON THE COVER:

In the large bowl: **BAKED ROASTED VEGGIE PASTA**, page 94.

On the side: **CHEESY BREAD**, page 66.

Cutlery available at Set Your Table in Lakewood, NJ and Monsey, NY. For additional sources for items used throughout this book, see page 126.

INTRODUCTION

LEAH: Baked ziti, penne à la vodka, and frozen pizza are probably the most frequently prepared dairy dinners.

VICTORIA: I think mac 'n cheese belongs up there too. And a Caesar salad on the side.

LEAH: I think we were all desperate and in need of some more options.

VICTORIA: Please! Especially since dairy dinners just make the whole family so ... happy. I'm the most popular mom when dinner is pizza or pasta.

LEAH: The weeks we were really in recipe testing mode, we ate only dairy. Except for Wednesday; that's the day my children's schools serve meat for lunch.

VICTORIA: I just made dairy every night.

LEAH: Well, you have fleish-phobia.[1]

[1] *The fear of eating meat. Those who suffer from fleish-phobia refrain from eating meat because they fear having a craving for dairy afterwards. In Jewish law, one must wait a specific time period between eating meat followed by dairy.*

VICTORIA: True. One day, at around noon, I was at our friend Renee Muller's house while she was baking Parmesan Crisps (page 44). Parmesan cheese for lunch, no problem. Then Leah walks in and we offer her the Crisps.

LEAH: I was already "meaty." I had a pastrami sandwich for lunch. I had to give up pastrami for a little while as we were writing this book so I could taste and test dairy.

VICTORIA: You never complained.

LEAH: Nope, no complaints. How could I complain when Cheesy Bread (page 66) is for lunch?

VICTORIA: So now you agree with me that cheese is a legitimate protein?

LEAH: I'm getting there. The only problem was the dairy desserts. Big problem. As food writers who need to be constantly testing and tasting, we each have our own ways of watching what we eat. Usually, I stay away from sweets and eat them only occasionally.

VICTORIA: I love dessert and will often skip a meal if I want something sweet instead of real food.

LEAH: When creating dairy desserts for this book, though, all it took was one taste and our strategies went out the window. There were too many delicious desserts around — so delicious you'd want to live on an island and be stranded with them. So how could I limit the desserts I ate? And how many meals could Victoria possibly skip?

VICTORIA: After one night of recipe testing, there was no milk left in the house for my children's breakfast. I opened the fridge, searching for a solution. And there it was! My Crème Brûlée (page 109) that I made with eggs, milk, and peanut butter. The perfect breakfast.

LEAH: Speaking of breakfast, there is no waffle recipe in the book. Why? I made so many versions. None were perfect. My children don't want to see another waffle for breakfast for a long time.

VICTORIA: Maybe you can serve them Crème Brûlée?

LEAH: I'm still on the search for crispy, crispy waffles with a fluffy inside. Don't send me a recipe — bring me one already prepared. Tasting is believing!

VICTORIA: We learned many things while writing this book. We met new people through our recipe searches and discovered lots of new flavors.

LEAH: But the most important thing we learned is that parve could never really be as good as dairy. Bring on the butter!

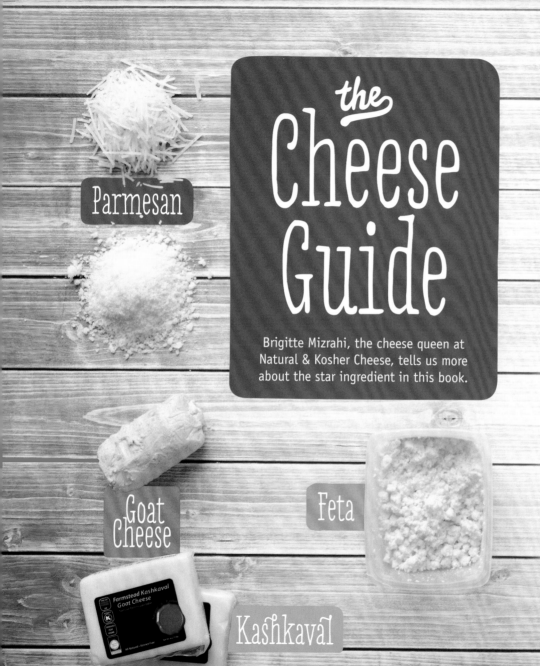

the Cheese Guide

Brigitte Mizrahi, the cheese queen at Natural & Kosher Cheese, tells us more about the star ingredient in this book.

Parmesan

Goat Cheese

Feta

Kashkaval

PARMESAN "It was a long process to produce top-quality kosher Parmesan. Parmesan is aged from one to two years, resulting in a cheese with a nutty and intense flavor," Brigitte tells us. Throughout this book, we love it shaved, grated, or shredded. (After eating this cheese, many have the custom to wait 6 hours before eating meat.)

GOAT CHEESE "Goat cheese is a fresh cheese that you can spread like cream cheese. Ours is a farmstead cheese, which means it's produced in the same place where the goats are milked." Natural & Kosher's goat cheese also comes in a variety of flavors. Spread this cinnamon and apple version over a baguette and add a drizzle of honey for a sweet brunch. Savory flavorings, such as za'atar or harissa, also complement plain goat cheese well.

FETA We use feta, shredded or crumbled, throughout this book; Brigitte tells us it's also fabulous over a pizza.

KASHKAVAL Goat Kashkaval is a sharp and flavorful hard cheese. Enjoy it along with wine. Grate or cube it and add it to a salad.

Fresh Mozzarella

Ciligine (small balls of fresh mozzarella)

Mozzarella

Cheddar

Pepper Jack

FRESH MOZZARELLA What's the difference between fresh mozzarella and regular mozzarella? "There's actually not much in common except the name," Brigitte told us. "Fresh is made from cooked cheese curds. It's sold as soon as it's made. It has a nice milky fresh taste, and is the stretchiest cheese available."

MOZZARELLA Mozzarella is made using rennet and draining out whey. It must be aged for a few weeks before slicing or shredding. N & K's Mozzarella sticks are the convenient choice for making stretchy mozzarella sticks or our Arancini on page 28.

PIZZA CHEESE What's pizza cheese made from? "It's usually a type of mozzarella. Ours is a hybrid between mozzarella and Monterey Jack [a semi-hard cheese]."

MUENSTER (not shown) "The Jewish people love Muenster. It reminds them of the cheeses they grew up with. Even though it's a hard cheese, it's mild and creamy. Lots of spices complement it and it melts very well."

CHEDDAR "It's amazing on scalloped potatoes or in a quiche. Pair it with apples on a cheese board or as a snack."

PEPPER JACK Pepper Jack is Monterey Jack with peppers. "It's a fun cheese. Use it in Nachos (for an extra kick, use it instead of mozzarella in ours on page 32). It's great inside a quesadilla."

BRIE Don't forget the brie! (not shown). "Brie is the king of cheeses and a staple on cheese boards. Enjoy it with pesto or jam and champagne. Bake it inside phyllo shells. You can warm it in the oven and scoop it out so it's gooey, then enjoy over toast with fruit. It's amazing with a little maple syrup for brunch."

Make It LiGHT

Dairy isn't usually known to be low in calories ... but here are a few recipe suggestions, plus some options and adaptations to make them even lighter.

Saturday Night Frittata, *page 14*

Use low-fat milk. Replace one of the whole eggs with 2 egg whites.

Granola Thins, *page 21*

Cold Brewed Coffee *and* Blended Coffee Frappe, *pages 22 and 23*

Use low-fat or fat-free milk and a sugar substitute.

Peach Cobbler Smoothie, *page 24*

Replace orange juice with water. Use a sugar substitute and Lite Vanilla Greek yogurt.

Green Shake, *page 24*

Broccoli Spring Roll, *page 30*

Bake according to instructions in step 4.

Roasted Veggie Galette, *page 36*

Use whole wheat white pastry flour. You can also use a rolling pin to make the dough thinner and top it with more veggies. You'll have a larger yield with less dough per serving.

Cauliflower Garlic Bites, *page 38*

Green Beans with Crispy Parmesan, *page 39*

Use half the quantity of Parmesan cheese.

Stuffed Sole, *page 42*

Omit the cheese.

Broccoli and Cheese Soup, *page 46*

Reduce the quantity of cheddar cheese according to taste.

French Mushroom Soup, *page 48*

Choose a light mozzarella cheese or use fewer croutons. Do not omit the butter; just a little bit affects the flavor of the whole pot.

Cauliflower Lemon Soup, *page 50*

Hot Asian Mushroom Salad, *page 52*

Use a sugar substitute and light feta cheese.

Pomegranate and Apple Salad with Creamy Parmesan, *page 54*

Use light mayonnaise (we always do) and a sugar substitute.

Sunflower Salad, *page 58*

Use light feta cheese; replace sunflower brittle with plain roasted salted sunflower seeds.

Eggplant Parmesan Wraps, *page 64*

You can bake or broil eggplant slices instead of breading and frying.

180 Calorie (or Less!) Cheesecake, *page 104*

Enjoy as is, or omit crust and use sugar substitute.

The Magic of Greek

Whether you're blending a smoothie (page 24), making a lighter cheesecake (page 104), or whipping up a creamy sauce, we discovered that Norman's Greek Yogurt is a magic ingredient for enjoying dairy without the calories. Using this chart, play around making lighter versions of your favorites.

1 CUP BUTTER = ¼ cup Greek yogurt + ½ cup butter

1 CUP OIL = ¾ cup Greek yogurt

1 CUP SOUR CREAM = 1 cup Greek yogurt

1 CUP MAYONNAISE = 1 cup Greek yogurt

1 CUP CREAM CHEESE = 1 cup Greek yogurt

1 CUP HEAVY CREAM = ½ cup Greek yogurt + ½ cup milk

Love cereal but want to cut calories and add protein to your breakfast? For a complete bowl of creaminess + crunch, I add just a couple of spoons of cereal to Greek yogurt. I like Rice Krispies or Cocoa Krispies in Norman's Lite Coffee Yogurt, or cornflakes in Norman's Vanilla Lite Greek Yogurt. –V.......

Load up Norman's plain or Strawberry Lite Greek yogurt with fresh fruit and just one spoonful of granola. It's portable as a meal-on-the-go, and much more filling and satisfying than the carb-filled cereal bowl. I love to add pomegranate in the winter and fresh peaches in the summer. –V.......

Make the Sauce

No Cook Pizza Sauce

I like to top my pizza with a thin No Cook Pizza Sauce that I stir together in a minute. Add a pinch of sugar, ½ teaspoon kosher salt, 1 teaspoon oregano, and 1 teaspoon garlic powder to a 15-ounce can of crushed tomatoes. —L.

Homemade Marinara

Make a double batch and freeze in small containers.

INGREDIENTS

2 Tbsp	olive oil or butter
1	large onion, diced
2	garlic cloves, crushed
2	(28-oz) cans crushed or whole tomatoes
1 tsp	dried basil
1 tsp	dried oregano
1 tsp	garlic powder
1 tsp	kosher salt
•	pinch coarse black pepper
2 tsp	sugar

I haven't bought a jar of marinara or pizza sauce in years. Homemade sauce is easy, inexpensive ... and tastes so much better. The secret is the cooking time ... as the sauce simmers, the tomatoes lose their acidity and sweeten. —V.

INSTRUCTIONS
YIELD 2 cups

1. Heat oil or melt butter in a large stockpot over medium-low heat. Add onions and garlic and sauté until onion is soft, about 7 minutes. Add crushed tomatoes and bring to a simmer. Add basil, oregano, garlic powder, salt, and pepper. Let cook for at least 30 minutes.

2. Stir in sugar. Using an immersion blender or in the jar of blender, blend the sauce until smooth.

Make the Cheese

Homemade Ricotta

There isn't always ricotta to be found in my town. I make this version all the time rather than change my dinner plans. –V.

YIELD 1 lb ricotta cheese

INGREDIENTS

1	half gallon whole milk
⅓ cup	vinegar

INSTRUCTIONS

1. Add milk to a large saucepan over medium heat. Bring to a simmer. Immediately stir in vinegar, turn off heat, and let sit for 5 minutes. The cheese curds will begin to separate from the whey.

2. Place a colander or sieve over a bowl and line with a cheesecloth or a double layer of paper towels. Ladle curds into colander and let drain until cheese thickens.

Homemade Cream Cheese

You may not ever need to make your own cheese if you live next door to a grocery. But if you run out of your cream cheese or ricotta, or you're the type who likes to "do it yourself," here are our two basic versions. Have fun and add your own additions, such as chopped scallions, herbs, or vegetables. –L.

YIELD 8 ounces

INGREDIENTS

1 lb	sour cream
¾ tsp	salt

INSTRUCTIONS

1. Combine sour cream and salt. Add to a cheesecloth and tie up over a faucet. Let drip for 8 to 12 hours.

2. Transfer cheese to a bowl and stir well. Cheese will stay fresh for up to a week.

MAKE IT!

Micro-Frittata

FOR the quickie version of our frittata (page 14), chop any vegetables you have in your fridge (no need to sauté first). Whisk in eggs, salt, and some cheese and add the mixture to a microwave-safe dish. Microwave for about 5 minutes, until mixture is set. No oil, frying pan, or oven needed!

Saturday Night Frittata	14	Granola Thins	21	Peach Cobbler Smoothie	24
Corn Muffins	16	Cold Brewed Iced Coffee	22	Green Shake	24
Chocolate Croissant Rolls	18	Hot Vanilla	22	Chocolate Chip Cookie Milkshake	25
Sour Cream Pancakes	20	Blended Coffee Frappe	23		

Breakfast

Saturday Night Frittata

INGREDIENTS

2 Tbsp	oil
½	onion, diced
2	eggs
2	egg whites
⅓ cup	milk
2-3 Tbsp	shredded cheese
½ tsp	kosher salt

INSTRUCTIONS

1. Preheat oven to 400°F.
2. Heat oil in an ovenproof frying pan over low heat. Add onion and sauté until golden, 10-12 minutes.
3. Meanwhile, in a small bowl, whisk together eggs, egg whites, milk, cheese, and salt.
4. Remove onions from frying pan and spray pan well with nonstick cooking spray. Return onions to pan and top with egg mixture. Bake for 10 minutes.
5. Use a silicone spatula to loosen the edges. Flip frittata onto a plate. Serve with crackers, rice cakes, or bread.

YIELD
1 frittata

Use up any veggies in your fridge by sautéing them with the onion.

If your frying pan has a plastic handle, cover it with foil before baking.

EVERY Motzei Shabbat, when I'm perfectly lazy on the couch, my husband asks, "Is there anything to eat?" What he really means is, "Can you make me a frittata?" I get up to sauté an onion, and then return to the couch. And then I forget about it until someone says, "Is something burning?" So after I pick out all the burned pieces, add the eggs, and pop the frittata in the oven, I return to the couch. Until someone asks again, "Is something burning?" So I fetch the well-done frittata, flip it onto a plate, serve it with some pita or crackers, and return to the couch. I hope it was worth the wait. Whether you enjoy yours for breakfast or on Saturday nights, don't burn yours too. –V.

Corn Muffins

INGREDIENTS

1½ cups	cornmeal
2½ cups	milk, minus 1 tablespoon
1 Tbsp	lemon juice
2 cups	flour
1 Tbsp	baking powder
1 tsp	kosher salt
⅔ cup	sugar
2	eggs
½ cup	oil
•	raw sugar, for sprinkling (optional)

INSTRUCTIONS

1. Preheat oven to 400°F. Grease muffin pan very well.

2. In a small bowl, combine cornmeal, milk, and lemon juice. Let stand 5 minutes.

3. In a large bowl, whisk together flour, baking powder, salt, and sugar. Mix in cornmeal mixture, eggs, and oil; stir until smooth.

4. Pour batter into prepared muffin cups, filling to the top. Sprinkle with raw sugar (optional).

5. Bake for 20-25 minutes or until tops are golden.

YIELD
14 muffins

Besides the great taste, we also love this recipe because it requires no mixer or melting butter.

At Milt's, a slice of cornbread is served next to savory dishes. For an even nicer presentation, sometimes it's baked in mini skillets.

I spent days and days making all different types of corn muffins. Leah and I both knew the flavor we were after. But even after all those batches, the perfect recipe was still elusive.

Then, after my husband ate at Milt's Barbecue for the Perplexed in Chicago, he put me in touch with the chef. Chef Bryan Gryka serves the parve version of this recipe as a cornbread alongside his famous barbecue dishes.

We knew the first time we tasted. This is the corn muffin we've both been searching for our entire lives. —V.

Chocolate Croissant Rolls

INGREDIENTS

DOUGH:

2½ cups	flour
¼ tsp	kosher salt
2½ tsp	instant dry yeast
¼ cup	sugar
2	eggs
¼ cup	(½ stick) butter, at room temperature
½ cup	orange juice

FLOUR/BUTTER MIXTURE:

½ cup	flour
¾ cup	(1½ sticks) butter, at room temperature

FILLING:

1	(3.5 oz) praline-filled chocolate bar, cut into matchsticks

If using fresh yeast, you'll need ¾ ounce.

INSTRUCTIONS

1. Prepare the dough: In the bowl of an electric mixer, combine flour and salt. Add yeast, sugar, eggs, butter, and orange juice. Dough should be slightly sticky (if it seems very sticky, add additional flour, 1 tablespoon at a time). Let dough rest ½ hour.

2. Meanwhile, prepare the flour/butter mixture: In a separate bowl, knead flour and butter together until combined. Set aside.

3. Preheat oven to 350°F. Line 2 baking sheets with parchment paper.

4. On a floured surface, roll dough into a rectangle. Smear flour/butter mixture over rectangle. Fold ⅓ of the dough from each side over the center, like a letter. Refrigerate 4-6 hours or up to overnight.

5. Divide dough in half. Roll each half into a 12-14-inch circle, trimming the edges if necessary. Slice into 8 or 12 wedges (like a pizza). On the widest end of each triangle, place one or two chocolate matchsticks. Fold end of dough over chocolate and roll very tightly, rugelach-style.

6. Place croissants on baking sheet and let rise 30 minutes. Bake for 15 minutes until golden brown.

YIELD
16 or 24 croissants

TIDBIT:
Legend has it that the croissant was invented after one of the great battles in Europe to celebrate the defeat of Arab forces trying to conquer Europe, with the pastry's curved shape representing the Islamic crescent.

ReAL flaky croissants take hours to make. My mother and aunts have been making this easier version for years instead. They have the flakiness of traditional croissants with the texture of a roll. With the addition of chocolate, you may as well add that latte and imagine you're enjoying breakfast in a European café. –L.

Sour Cream Pancakes

INGREDIENTS

2	eggs
1 cup	sour cream OR 250 grams soft cheese
10 Tbsp	flour
7 Tbsp	sugar
1 tsp	vanilla extract
¼ cup	milk

YIELD 18-20 small pancakes

I'M lucky to be blessed with lots of brothers and brothers-in-law. Then they get married and I get fabulous new sisters-in-law. And then they share recipes with me. Thanks, Chevy, for this super breakfast and brunch pancake that's really good even at room temperature. —L.

INSTRUCTIONS

1. In a medium bowl, whisk together eggs, sour cream, flour, sugar, vanilla, and milk.

2. Grease a nonstick griddle or frying pan, or heat a pancake maker. Scoop 2 tablespoons batter at a time onto the hot griddle and cook for 2-3 minutes per side, until golden brown.

Granola Thins

INGREDIENTS

2 cups	quick-cooking oats
1	egg
¼ cup	(½ stick) butter, melted
1 Tbsp	brown sugar
2 Tbsp	honey
½ tsp	vanilla extract
¼ tsp	cinnamon
1	(3.5 oz) bar bittersweet chocolate, chopped

YIELD 16 squares

I'M still trying to figure out the best way to store these. Should you keep them in an airtight container at room temperature (if you like them chewy)? Or in a tin in the freezer (if you like them crunchy)? It doesn't really matter, because these tend to get eaten up while they're still cooling. —L.

INSTRUCTIONS

1. Preheat oven to 350°F. In a large bowl, combine oats, egg, butter, brown sugar, honey, vanilla, and cinnamon.

2. Place mixture between 2 sheets of parchment paper. Using a rolling pin, roll as thin as possible into a rectangle. Remove top paper. Transfer mixture with parchment paper to baking sheet and bake for 10-15 minutes, until crispy at the edges.

3. Meanwhile, melt the chocolate. Using an offset spatula, spread chocolate as thinly as possible over the warm granola thins. Let cool for 5 minutes as chocolate sets. Using a pizza slicer or sharp knife, cut into squares.

To melt chocolate, microwave for 1 minute. Stir. Microwave for 30 seconds. Stir again until smooth. Microwave for 15 additional seconds if necessary.

Breakfast Drinks

Cold Brewed Iced Coffee

INGREDIENTS

3 cups   cold water
⅓ cup   ground coffee
2½ cups milk
  •   sweetener,
         to taste

YIELD 6 servings

THIS is the trendy coffee right now, and it's totally worth the hype. When coffee is brewed cold instead of hot, it's not bitter and even needs less sweetener. I take a little bit from the jar each day when making myself an iced coffee or frappe, or, for company, I make a huge batch and serve it in a beverage cooler.   –V.

INSTRUCTIONS

1. Prepare the coffee base: In a container or jar, combine water and coffee. Using a spoon, stir to combine. Seal and leave at room temperature for 12 hours.

2. Place a colander over a second container. Line colander with paper towels or a coffee filter. Strain the coffee mixture through the colander. If necessary, strain again if it seems that some of the grounds have passed through the towels or filter.

3. To prepare the entire amount, combine coffee base with milk and sweetener to taste. To prepare individual cups, combine equal parts coffee and milk; add sweetener to taste. Serve over ice. Coffee base will keep in the refrigerator for 2 to 3 weeks.

Hot Vanilla

INGREDIENTS

2 cups   milk
2½ Tbsp   sugar
1 tsp   vanilla extract

YIELD 2 cups

WHEN my kids come in from the cold, they snub hot cocoa. This is their first request instead.   –V.

INSTRUCTIONS

• In a small saucepan over medium heat, combine milk, sugar, and vanilla. Cook until hot but not boiling. Pour into mugs.

Blended Coffee Frappe

For a flavored frappe, you can also use ¼ teaspoon vanilla or almond extract or 1 tablespoon instant vanilla pudding powder.

INGREDIENTS

- *1 cup* ice
- *1 cup* milk
- *1 cup* strong brewed coffee
- • sweetener, to taste
- *1-3* pumps flavored syrup, optional

INSTRUCTIONS

- Combine ice, milk, coffee, sweetener, and flavored syrup if desired. Blend until smooth.

YIELD 1 frappe

IN the summer, this is my twice-a-day staple. You don't need a visit to the coffee shop for a perfect (low-cal!) frappe. —V.

Breakfast Shakes

Peach Cobbler Smoothie

INGREDIENTS

1 cup	orange juice
1½ cups	frozen peaches
1 Tbsp	sugar or 3 packets sugar substitute
1	(6-oz) container (¾ cup) vanilla Greek yogurt
½ tsp	cinnamon (optional)

YIELD 1 large or 2 small smoothies

IF using fresh peaches in the summertime, add some ice. But don't wait for summer to enjoy this protein-packed breakfast on the go. To cut calories, you can substitute water for the orange juice.
—V.

INSTRUCTIONS

- Combine orange juice, peaches, yogurt, sugar, and cinnamon. Blend until smooth. Will keep, refrigerated, for 2-3 days.

How do you measure frozen peaches? Add orange juice to the blender first. Add peaches until liquid reaches the 2½ cup mark.

We like to use Norman's Lite Vanilla Greek Yogurt, so my smoothie doesn't have added sugar. If you're using plain Greek yogurt, add 1 tablespoon vanilla extract and 1 tablespoon vanilla pudding powder.

Green Shake

INGREDIENTS

1 cup	almond, soy, or coconut milk
1 cup	water
1	banana
1 cup	frozen berries
2 cups	fresh baby spinach

YIELD 6 cups
INSPIRED BY COOKKOSHER MEMBER BabyBearHugs

THIS is a light and refreshing drink that'll make you feel healthy and energized. When blending leafy greens, the Vitamix really does the job right.
—L.

INSTRUCTIONS

1. In the jar of a blender, combine milk and water. Add banana, berries, and spinach.
2. Blend until smooth.

Chocolate Chip Cookie Milkshake

INGREDIENTS

4 scoops	vanilla or cookie dough ice cream (1 cup packed)
3	chocolate chip cookies
½ cup	milk
1 tsp	vanilla extract

INSTRUCTIONS

- In the jar of a blender, combine ice cream, cookies, milk, and vanilla. Blend. Enjoy immediately.

YIELD   1 milkshake

ONE of my favorite Florida food memories is enjoying the chocolate chip cookie milkshake from Sara's. And so, on a snowy Sunday afternoon in New Jersey, I brought my family back on vacation, even if just for a few sips.   —V.

MAKE IT!

Customize Your Quiche

USE our Three-Cheese Quiche (page 34) as a base for any type of veggie quiche. You'll only need half the dough, to make the bottom crust. Add your veggies to the cheese mixture and omit the top crust. We added different colored grape tomatoes and topped the quiche with fresh or dried basil.

Starters *and* Sides

Arancini

INGREDIENTS

1 cup	uncooked sushi rice
1	egg, lightly beaten
¼ tsp	Italian seasoning or dried oregano
2 Tbsp	shredded mozzarella cheese
¼ tsp	kosher salt
•	pinch coarse black pepper
4	mozzarella cheese sticks, cut into ¾-inch cubes

COATING:

1	egg
½ cup	finely crushed flavored cornflake crumbs
•	oil, for frying

Don't want to use lots of oil? Deep fry in a small saucepan. You'll be able to fry 3 balls at a time.

INSTRUCTIONS

1. Prepare rice according to package directions (do not add rice vinegar). While warm, stir in egg, seasoning, and shredded cheese; stir to combine. Season with salt and pepper. Cool; refrigerate rice until cold. The rice should have a sticky texture.

2. With wet hands, scoop up about 1 tablespoon of rice. Form a ball and flatten it. Place a mozzarella cube in the center and press firmly to form into a ball again; roll between your palms to compress the ball tightly. Repeat with remaining rice. Place balls in freezer for 10 minutes to become firm.

3. Prepare the coating: Lightly beat egg in a shallow dish. Place cornflake crumbs into a second shallow dish. Roll rice balls in egg, then in crumbs. Arancini can be prepared ahead, frozen at this point, and fried fresh, after thawing for about 10 minutes.

4. Heat oil in a deep fryer at 350°F or in saucepan over medium-high heat. When oil is hot, fry balls until brown and crispy, about 3 minutes. Serve alongside warm marinara sauce or a mixture of marinara and cream.

YIELD
18-20 balls

TIDBIT:
In its true form, Parmigiano-Reggiano must carry a Protected Designation of Origin certification. The certification guarantees that the cheese is produced exclusively in the region of northern Italy where it was first developed.

Arancini (a·ran·tchee´·nee) are rice balls. The Italian word "arancini" means "little orange," referring to the shape and color of these rice balls.

ONE evening, I met my sister-in-law at a restaurant. I was running a little late and she had already done all the ordering. I saw these on the table and thought they were mozzarella balls. I dug right in ... and was surprised to find ... rice! To me, rice was a side dish for a meat meal, not a filling for a cheesy dairy appetizer. But by the time I finished my first Arancini, I was won over.

Traditional Arancini are made using risotto rice. But if you're more likely to have sushi rice in your pantry (like me), it makes the perfect substitute. —L.

We cut up Natural & Kosher's Mozzarella Sticks for a stretchy, gooey cheesiness inside our balls.

Broccoli Spring Rolls

INGREDIENTS

4 cups	frozen broccoli florets, completely thawed
½ cup	finely diced onions
2 Tbsp	cream cheese
2 Tbsp	shredded cheddar or mozzarella cheese
½ tsp	kosher salt
•	pinch coarse black pepper
8-10	spring roll wrappers
•	oil, for frying

Want to make your own cream cheese? See page 11.

INSTRUCTIONS

1. Chop broccoli very finely. Once thawed and chopped, the broccoli should yield 2 cups.

2. In a small bowl, combine broccoli, onions, cream cheese, shredded cheese, salt, and pepper.

3. Place a spring roll wrapper on your work surface. Place approximately 3 tablespoons filling across the center of the wrapper. Fold in the two sides, then fold the bottom half of the wrapper over the filling. Roll up to completely enclose. Use water to seal if necessary. Spring rolls can be frozen at this point.

4. Heat oil in a saucepan. Add spring rolls and fry until golden, about 3-4 minutes per side. Alternatively, spring rolls can be baked at 425°F for 18 minutes or until crispy.

YIELD
8-10 spring rolls

What's the difference between spring roll wrappers and egg roll wrappers? Egg roll wrappers contain egg in the dough and are much heavier. Spring roll wrappers are light and crispy when fried. We use the spring roll wrappers made from wheat, not the delicate rice paper wrappers.

I love making and serving spring rolls but sometimes I don't like the fact that I have to precook the filling. So if I have a problem, I solve it! Here is a spring roll that needs no precooking. Chop, fill, and fry!   –L.

White Nachos

INGREDIENTS

WHITE CHEESE SAUCE:

1 Tbsp	butter
½ cup	heavy cream
½ cup	shredded mozzarella cheese
¼ tsp	kosher salt

TOMATO SALAD:

1	large tomato, finely diced
2 Tbsp	olive oil
½	small red onion, finely diced
¾ tsp	kosher salt
¼ tsp	coarse black pepper

MASHED AVOCADO:

1	ripe avocado
1 Tbsp	lemon juice
½ tsp	kosher salt
⅛ tsp	coarse black pepper

- white corn chips

INSTRUCTIONS

1. Prepare the cheese sauce: Melt butter in a sauté pan over low heat. Add heavy cream and mozzarella cheese. Bring to a simmer and cook until cream thickens and cheese is melted. Season with salt.

2. Prepare the tomato salad: In a small bowl, combine tomato, olive oil, red onion, salt, and pepper. Set aside.

3. Prepare the mashed avocado: In a small bowl, mash the avocado with lemon juice, salt, and pepper.

4. Serve hot white cheese sauce, tomato salad, and mashed avocado in three small bowls alongside white corn chips.

YIELD
4 servings

Pre-shredded cheese is coated in starch to prevent the strands from sticking together. But since the starch also interferes with the melting process, for best ooey gooey cheesy results, use freshly shredded cheese.

If not serving immediately, you can heat the sauce by placing it in a ramekin and zapping in the microwave for 20-30 seconds until hot.

IF there's one thing I don't like about nachos, it's when the cheese hardens on the chips. In this version, the cheese is a dip. You can keep on dipping ... and there's no hard cheese. And even better ... no soggy chips. With the simple additions of tomato salad and avocado, it's a great party food.   —L.

Three-Cheese Quiche

INGREDIENTS

CRUST:

⅞ cup	(1¾ sticks) butter, at room temperature
2½ cups	flour
1	(16-oz) container sour cream or (250 grams) leben

FILLING:

3	(8.8-oz) containers 5% or 9% soft cheese
8.8 oz	feta or Bulgarian cheese
2 cups	shredded Muenster or other hard cheese
1 tsp	sugar
3	eggs
3 Tbsp	flour
1	egg, beaten
•	sesame seeds, for sprinkling

INSTRUCTIONS

1. Prepare the crust: In a large bowl, combine butter, flour, and sour cream. Knead until smooth (it will yield a sticky dough). You can also use an electric mixer. Wrap dough ball in plastic wrap and refrigerate for 8 hours.

2. Prepare the filling: In a large bowl, combine cheeses, sugar, eggs, and flour.

3. Preheat oven to 350°F. Grease a 10-inch deep round baking pan.

4. Divide dough in half. Roll out one half into a 16-inch circle. Place dough into prepared baking pan to cover the bottom and sides. Pour in filling. Roll remaining dough into a 12-inch circle. Place over filling; press to secure edges to the sides. Cut away any excess dough.

5. Cut slits into the dough. Brush with beaten egg. Sprinkle liberally with sesame seeds. Bake for 60 minutes, until golden. Serve hot or at room temperature.

YIELD

8-10 servings

INSPIRED BY COOKKOSHER MEMBER
CookRight

See how we create variations of this quiche in "Make It!" on page 26.

THE quiches I grew up with never had a crust and always were made of spinach or squash (as featured in *Passover Made Easy*). And I didn't even call them quiches, but the Arabic term, *jiben*. For a real crusty, cheesy quiche, we tapped Leah's family recipe books instead. This tested-and-true version has been a mainstay on her mother-in-law's table for decades. Prepare it ahead, freeze it, bake fresh, and pamper your guests with the ultimate dairy side dish.

–V.

Roasted Veggie Galette

INGREDIENTS

1	zucchini, diced
1	sweet potato, diced
1	small eggplant, diced
1	red onion, diced
1	red pepper, diced
3 Tbsp	oil
½ tsp	kosher salt
•	pinch coarse black pepper

DOUGH:

2¼ cups	flour
2 Tbsp	sugar
1 tsp	kosher salt
2 tsp	dry yeast
⅔ cup	water
¼ cup	oil
⅓ cup	shredded mozzarella cheese
1	egg, beaten

INSTRUCTIONS

1. Preheat oven to 425°F. On a large baking sheet, toss zucchini, sweet potato, eggplant, onion, and pepper with oil, salt, and pepper. Spread in a single layer. Bake for 30 minutes.

2. Meanwhile, prepare the dough: In a large bowl, combine flour, sugar, salt, yeast, water, and oil. Stir to combine; then, using your hands, knead until dough is smooth (the dough will come together quickly and will not require much kneading). If the dough seems a bit dry, add a drop of water. Cover and let rise for 20 minutes.

3. Lower oven temperature to 375°F. Roll dough on a piece of parchment paper into a 12-inch circle. Transfer to a baking sheet. Place the roasted vegetables in the center, leaving a 1-inch border. Fold edges of the dough towards the center. Sprinkle vegetables with cheese. Brush crust with beaten egg and bake for 20 minutes.

You'll want to dice your sweet potato a little smaller than the other veggies so they all roast evenly.

YIELD
1 large or 4 small pies

You can use white whole wheat flour for a galette with a more rustic taste.

Make one large galette and serve pie-style or customize mini galettes for each person (i.e., for each picky kid).

ANY other galette dough you'll find is made with lots of sticks of margarine or butter. I love galettes but didn't like that. Once this version was perfected, it became my go-to dish when I haven't gone shopping, since I can really use whatever veggies I have in the fridge.

Just don't tell my kids it's called a galette. I sell it as a "cheesy pie."

—V.

Cauliflower Garlic Bites

INGREDIENTS

1	(24-oz) bag frozen cauliflower
1 Tbsp	olive oil
¼ tsp	kosher salt
⅛ tsp	coarse black pepper

GARLIC DRESSING:

1 Tbsp	olive oil
1½ Tbsp	grated Parmesan cheese
1½ tsp	lemon juice
3	garlic cloves, minced
1 tsp	dried parsley
½ tsp	kosher salt

YIELD   4 servings

I fell in love with cauliflower when we made a spicy version in *Starters & Sides Made Easy*. Now, Parmesan and garlic add that savory flavor to our blank canvas. Imagine a carb-free garlic knot!   –L.

INSTRUCTIONS

1. Preheat oven to 400°F. Grease a baking sheet with nonstick cooking spray or line with parchment paper.

2. Add cauliflower to baking sheet. Drizzle with olive oil and season with salt and pepper. Bake for 35-40 minutes.

3. Prepare the garlic dressing: In a large bowl, combine olive oil, Parmesan cheese, lemon juice, garlic, parsley, and salt. Add hot cauliflower to bowl and toss to combine. Serve immediately.

To prepare this in advance, roast the cauliflower and prepare the dressing (store at room temperature). Then, warm cauliflower before serving and toss with sauce.

Green Beans with Crunchy Parmesan

INGREDIENTS

2 lb	green beans
1 Tbsp	oil (or nonstick cooking spray)
1 tsp	kosher salt
3	garlic cloves, minced
6 Tbsp	grated Parmesan cheese

YIELD   6 servings

THE trick of these green beans is to bake the Parmesan separately from the green beans. That way, everything gets crispy and crunchy.

–V.

If you're halving the recipe, you can do it all on one baking sheet.

INSTRUCTIONS

1. Preheat oven to 375°F. Grease a baking sheet. Line a second baking sheet with parchment paper.

2. Add green beans to greased baking sheet and toss with oil, salt, and garlic. Spread in a single layer. Bake for 10 minutes.

3. Sprinkle Parmesan cheese on lined baking sheet. Bake for 10 minutes, until cheese is golden and crispy (you can bake both baking sheets at the same time). Let cool and crumble into small bits (like breadcrumbs). Toss with green beans.

Sweet Chili Home Fries

INGREDIENTS

2½ lb	yellow potatoes (about 6-8), cubed
6 Tbsp	(¾ stick) butter
1 tsp	flour
1 cup	sweet chili sauce
•	kosher salt, for sprinkling
2	scallions, chopped

YIELD 4-5 servings

SATISFYING, sweet, spicy home fries.
-L.

INSTRUCTIONS

1. Bring a large pot of water to boil. Add potatoes and boil for 8-10 minutes to partially cook. Drain well and pat dry.

2. Heat oil in a deep fryer to 350°F or in a saucepan over medium-high heat. Add potatoes and fry for 6-8 minutes, or until golden. Transfer to a paper towel-lined plate.

3. Melt butter in a small saucepan over medium heat. Whisk in flour. Add sweet chili sauce and cook for 2-3 minutes.

4. In a large bowl, toss hot potatoes with sweet chili sauce mixture. Sprinkle with salt. Garnish with chopped scallions.

Crashed Potatoes

INGREDIENTS

2 lb	small red potatoes
3-4 Tbsp	olive oil
2 Tbsp	butter
1 tsp	kosher salt
¼ tsp	dried basil
¼ tsp	garlic powder
6 Tbsp	shredded mozzarella cheese

YIELD 4 servings

SMASHED potatoes + cheese = Crashed potatoes.

-L.

INSTRUCTIONS

1. Add potatoes to a large pot of water over high heat. Bring water to a boil. Boil for 20 minutes, until readily pierced by a fork.

2. Meanwhile, preheat oven to 425°F. Grease a baking sheet.

3. Drain potatoes and place on baking sheet. Using a potato masher, smash down on each potato. Drizzle with olive oil and dot with butter. Season with salt, basil, and garlic. Sprinkle with shredded cheese. Bake for 15 minutes, until edges are brown and crispy.

Stuffed Sole

INGREDIENTS

FILLING:

1 Tbsp	butter
⅓ cup	chopped shallots
⅓ cup	chopped baby bella mushrooms
½ cup	chopped frozen broccoli, thawed
⅓ cup	cooked brown rice
½ cup	shredded mozzarella cheese
2 Tbsp	lemon juice
¼ tsp	kosher salt
•	pinch black pepper

1½ lb	sole or flounder fillets
1 Tbsp	butter, melted
2 Tbsp	lemon juice
½ tsp	kosher salt
•	pinch coarse black pepper
•	pinch paprika

INSTRUCTIONS

1. Preheat oven to 350°F.
2. Prepare the filling: Melt 1 tablespoon butter in a sauté pan over medium heat. Add shallots and mushrooms and cook until softened, 5 minutes. Add broccoli and cook an additional 5 minutes. Stir in rice, cheese, and lemon juice. Season with salt and pepper.
3. Split fillets in half lengthwise. Place about 2 tablespoons filling at the end of each piece and roll up. Place in a baking pan.
4. Drizzle melted butter and lemon juice over fish. Season with paprika, salt, and pepper. Bake for 20 minutes.

YIELD

4-6 servings

INSPIRED BY COOKKOSHER MEMBER

Malkieh

If you don't like either mushrooms or broccoli, double up on the other veggie.

We didn't include other fish recipes in this book because, like many people, Victoria has the custom not to cook fish with dairy. But if there's going to be one elegant fish appetizer that makes the best use of butter and cheese, here it is. We couldn't believe how easy it was to make a dish that looks so beautiful. —L.

MAKE IT!

Soup Toppers

SOUP'S always more fun when there's a little bonus. You can mix and match any of our soup garnishes to add to your bowl. To make Parmesan Crisps, as pictured on our Broccoli and Cheddar Soup (page 46), line a baking sheet with parchment paper. Top with mounds of grated or shredded Parmesan cheese and bake at 375°F for about 8 minutes, until golden and crisp. The photo of our Cauliflower Lemon Soup (page 50) features a baguette skewer. Thread thin slices of baguette onto a skewer. Top with mozzarella and bake until cheese is melted. Here, we've topped our soup with a crispy wonton. Brush round wonton wrappers with butter and your choices of spices. Bake until crisp.

Soup, Salads and Sandwiches

Broccoli and Cheddar Soup with Parmesan Crisps

INGREDIENTS

1 Tbsp	olive oil
1	onion, diced
1	garlic clove, crushed
16 oz	frozen broccoli florets
1	potato, peeled and diced
4 cups	vegetable broth
6 oz	cheddar cheese, grated
¼ cup	buttermilk (OR ¼ cup milk and 1 tsp vinegar)
1½ tsp	kosher salt
•	pinch coarse black pepper

PARMESAN CRISPS:

¾ cup	shredded or grated Parmesan cheese

INSTRUCTIONS

1. Heat oil in a medium saucepan over medium heat. Add onion and garlic and sauté until onion is soft, 5-7 minutes.

2. Add broccoli, potato, and broth. Raise heat and bring to a boil. Lower heat and simmer for 7 minutes. Using an immersion blender, blend soup until smooth and creamy (if using a traditional blender, return soup to the pot after blending).

3. Stir in cheddar cheese and buttermilk. Stir until cheese is melted. Season with salt and pepper. Keep soup warm over low heat until ready to serve.

4. Prepare the Parmesan Crisps: Preheat oven to 375°F. Line a baking sheet with parchment paper. Spray parchment paper with 12 small circles of nonstick cooking spray. Scoop 1 tablespoon Parmesan cheese onto each circle and flatten into a round cracker shape. Bake for 8 minutes, until golden and crisp. Serve crisps alongside soup, or break up and sprinkle into soup bowl.

YIELD
6 servings

For more soup garnish ideas, see "Make It!" on page 44.

For Parmesan Crisps that look like this, use Natural & Kosher's shredded Parmesan cheese.

A while back, I went into the commercial kitchen of a dairy restaurant to watch the chefs prepare some of their dishes ... and was witness to the quantity of heavy cream that was used in each one. The soups definitely got their fair share, and of course they were delicious. But this soup (and the rest of them in this section) prove that making a delicious dairy and creamy soup doesn't require loads of cream.   –L.

French Mushroom Soup

INGREDIENTS

2 Tbsp	butter
1	large onion, cut into thin strips
8 oz	baby bella mushrooms, cleaned and sliced
5 cups	vegetable broth
1 cup	milk
1 tsp	kosher salt
2 cups	croutons
6 oz	sliced mozzarella cheese

If you keep parve consommé powder in your pantry, that works, too, as a substitution for the vegetable broth.

INSTRUCTIONS

1. Melt butter in a medium pot over low heat. Add onion and sauté until golden, 10-12 minutes. Add mushrooms and continue to cook until soft, 5-7 additional minutes.

2. Add vegetable broth and bring to a boil. Simmer for 20 minutes. Stir in milk and season with salt.

3. Add croutons to the surface of the soup. Layer cheese over the croutons. Simmer for an additional 10 minutes, or until cheese is melted (some of the cheese will melt into the soup and the rest will remain on top). Serve by ladling the soup and some of the crouton/cheese topping into each bowl.

YIELD
6 servings

Onion- and garlic-flavored croutons work great, but don't choose a crouton with herbs for this recipe. You'll also want to use standard-sized croutons, not the mini ones.

I own lots of kitchen gadgets and serving dishes, but I don't own soup crocks. And since I think there are some other people out there who also don't own those oven-friendly soup crocks, use my tricks for making a French-style soup all in the pot. (There's no need to melt the cheese on top of each bowl of soup under a broiler.) But, after all these years of the same one-pot Thursday night onion soup, my family was ready for a change. Now, we're enjoying this creamy, hearty, and easy mushroom version. Don't leave out the butter.   –V.

Cauliflower Lemon Soup

INGREDIENTS

2 Tbsp	butter
1	onion, diced
1	(24-oz) bag frozen cauliflower florets
4 cups	vegetable broth
1 cup	milk
1 tsp	kosher salt
•	juice of ½ lemon

INSTRUCTIONS

1. Melt butter in a large saucepan over low heat. Add onion and sauté until golden, about 12 minutes. Add cauliflower and cook an additional 2 minutes.

2. Add broth and bring to a boil. Simmer for 20 minutes.

3. Using a blender (or using an immersion blender right in the pot), blend soup until smooth. Return soup to pot. Stir in milk and salt. Continue to cook until soup thickens. Add lemon juice and stir to combine.

YIELD
6 servings

Is your lemon hard to squeeze? That could be because you're grabbing cold lemons from the fridge. Zap your lemon in the microwave for easy squeezing.

To learn how we make this garnish and others in the book, see "Make It!" on page 44.

WHENEVER I meet new people, I always ask what they've made for dinner recently. While I was in Miami for a food demonstration, I met Yvette Falack, who told me that she prepares cream of cauliflower soup and adds just a bit of lemon juice at the end. She said that little bit goes a long way in brightening up the flavor of the entire potful. When I returned home, I tried it. And Yvette was right. When dinner was over, I was scraping up the last bits left in the bottom of that pot.   —V.

How did we get our baguette skewers to be so creamy? We topped them with slices of Natural & Kosher's Fresh Mozzarella Cheese.

Hot Asian Mushroom Salad

INGREDIENTS

1 Tbsp	oil
8 oz	baby bella mushrooms, sliced
1 Tbsp	teriyaki sauce
1 head	Romaine lettuce, chopped
8-10	grape or cherry tomatoes, halved
½	red onion, thinly sliced
1½ oz	feta cheese

DRESSING:

2 Tbsp	oil
1 Tbsp	sugar
1	garlic clove, crushed
•	pinch kosher salt
¼ tsp	mustard

INSTRUCTIONS

1. Heat oil in a sauté pan over medium heat. Add mushrooms and sauté until soft, about 6 minutes. Add teriyaki sauce and cook an additional 1-2 minutes.

2. In a large salad bowl, combine lettuce, tomatoes, and red onion. Top with warm mushrooms.

3. Prepare the dressing: In a small bowl, whisk together oil, sugar, garlic, salt, and mustard. Toss with salad.

4. Using a box grater, shred the feta cheese directly over the salad.

YIELD
4 servings

Use either side of a box grater to shred your feta. When feta is finely shredded, you don't need much.

I thought that I didn't like feta cheese on my salads. Then, when eating lunch in one restaurant, I was served a salad with shredded cheese on top. Thinking it was mozzarella, I dug right in and loved it, later learning that I had just enjoyed my first feta cheese salad. Turns out, I like my feta cheese ... if it's shredded, not crumbled. Could it be that the consistency affects the taste? I think so.   –L.

Pomegranate and Apple Salad with Creamy Parmesan

INGREDIENTS

1	head Romaine lettuce, chopped
1	apple, diced or sliced
•	seeds of ½ pomegranate
1	grapefruit, supremed
2 Tbsp	finely diced red onion

DRESSING:

¼ cup	light mayonnaise
2 Tbsp	apple cider vinegar
1 Tbsp	water
1 tsp	sugar
1 tsp	kosher salt
•	pinch coarse black pepper
2 Tbsp	grated Parmesan cheese

INSTRUCTIONS

1. In a large bowl, combine lettuce, apple, pomegranate seeds, grapefruit, and red onion.

2. Prepare the dressing: In a small bowl, whisk together mayonnaise, vinegar, water, sugar, salt, pepper, and Parmesan cheese. Toss dressing with salad.

This salad is a big reason to keep your fridge stocked with Natural & Kosher's grated Parmesan Cheese ... other reasons include Cauliflower Garlic Bites (page 38), Green Beans with Crispy Parmesan (page 39), and our Avocado and Basil Pasta Salad (page 92).

YIELD
4 servings

Be sure to supreme your grapefruit, removing the bitter white membranes as you peel with a knife.

I often use apples instead of croutons in a salad. They give a similar crunch, but are lighter and add a refreshing flavor.

SOME salads come about very naturally. During the entire winter, when my refrigerator was full of apples and pomegranates, this was the default salad that I served at every dairy dinner. I never really measured or thought about it. I just threw things we loved into a bowl (and then Leah convinced me to throw in a supremed grapefruit too). It was always finished to the last leaf. So I suppose it's time to measure and write it down.   –V.

Grilled Cheese Toast Salad

INGREDIENTS

1	head Romaine lettuce, chopped
1	Persian cucumber, peeled and diced, or sliced into ribbons
½	red bell pepper, diced
15-20	cherry tomatoes, halved

PESTO MAYO DRESSING:

½ cup	light mayonnaise
2 Tbsp	oil
3 Tbsp	chopped fresh basil (½ cup loosely packed leaves) OR 9 frozen basil cubes
2½ Tbsp	lemon juice
2-3	garlic cloves
½ tsp	kosher salt
1-2 Tbsp	water

CHEESE TOAST CROUTONS:

1	(8-10 in) baguette
1½ Tbsp	pesto mayo dressing, above
3 Tbsp	shredded OR 1 slice mozzarella cheese

INSTRUCTIONS

1. In a large bowl, combine lettuce, cucumber, pepper, and tomatoes.

2. Prepare the dressing: In a mini chopper or using an immersion blender, combine mayonnaise, oil, basil, lemon juice, garlic, and salt. Gradually add water, as needed, to thin dressing slightly.

3. Prepare the croutons: Preheat oven or toaster oven to 400°F. Slice open baguette and spread with pesto mayo. Top with cheese. Close baguette and press down very well. Bake for 8-10 minutes (or 5-6 minutes in a toaster oven) until cheese is melted and bread is toasted. Using a pizza slicer, slice baguette into bite-sized croutons.

4. Add dressing to salad and toss to combine. Top with croutons.

Choose a baguette that's still soft when you squeeze it, as you'll be toasting it in the oven to make it crispier. The middle section of the baguette will work better than the ends for these croutons.

YIELD
4 servings

Persian cucumber and English cucumbers are both thin-skinned, nearly seedless, and can be used interchangeably in recipes. Since English cucumbers are much larger, though, you'll only need one-third to one-half if substituting.

Have extra dressing? Use it as a spread in your panini sandwiches or as a dip for your vegetables.

CAN'T decide between salad and grilled cheese for lunch? Now you can have both. Croutons aren't just the extra thing you throw into the salad for crunch. They are why you want to eat this salad!　　　　　−L.

Sunflower Salad

INGREDIENTS

1	head Romaine lettuce, chopped OR 5 cups baby spinach leaves
2	mangos, peeled and diced
½	red onion, finely diced

DRESSING:

4 oz	goat or feta cheese
2 Tbsp	olive oil
2 Tbsp	white wine vinegar
½ tsp	Italian seasoning

SUNFLOWER BRITTLE:

1 Tbsp	butter
¼ cup	salted hulled sunflower seeds
¼ cup	sugar

You can omit the Italian seasoning if you're using Natural & Kosher's Herbed Goat Cheese.

INSTRUCTIONS

1. In a large bowl, combine lettuce, mango, and red onion. Set aside.

2. Prepare the dressing: In a small bowl, use a fork to mash goat cheese with olive oil, vinegar, and Italian seasoning. You can also use a mini chopper for a smoother consistency.

3. Prepare the brittle: Melt butter in a sauté pan over medium heat. Add sunflower seeds and toast for 30-60 seconds. Remove from pan and set aside. Add sugar to the pan and stir constantly until sugar is melted, about 3 minutes. It should be brown and completely smooth. Stir in sunflower seeds, pour into a thin layer onto a sheet of parchment paper, and flatten as much as possible. Let harden. Chop to small bits, using a mini chopper or the bottom of a can.

4. Toss salad with dressing. Top with sunflower brittle.

For a light version, use light feta cheese and salted sunflower seeds without the glaze.

YIELD
4 servings

You can also use this easy no-candy-thermometer technique to make candy brittle using any kind of nut.

Both goat cheese and feta cheese are naturally salty cheeses, so you won't need additional salt in this salad.

LEAH is always trying to convince me that not every single salad needs to be super-low-calorie. She knows I'm always trying to keep them light so I can save my calories for dessert. But this salad comes with dessert built in. With saltiness, sweetness, and creaminess in each bite, I'm completely satisfied. —V.

Hasselback Baguette

INGREDIENTS

2 Tbsp	oil
1	small red onion, diced
1	red bell pepper, diced
½ tsp	dried basil
¼ tsp	kosher salt
•	pinch coarse black pepper
1	(24-in) baguette
•	shredded cheese

EQUIPMENT:

3	long wooden skewers

You can experiment with different cheeses inside your Hasselback Baguettes. We like Natural & Kosher's Mexican blend.

INSTRUCTIONS

1. Preheat oven to 475°F. Line a baking sheet with parchment paper.

2. Heat oil in a sauté pan over medium heat. Add onion and sauté for 3-4 minutes. Add pepper and sauté for an additional 3 minutes. Season with basil, salt, and pepper.

3. Cut off the ends of the baguette; discard ends or reserve for another purpose. Slice baguette into 1½-inch thick slices (you should have about 15 slices). Slit each slice ¾ through the top, leaving the lower end uncut.

4. Thread each skewer through uncut (lower) part of 5 slices. Add vegetable mixture and cheese into each slit. Place skewers onto prepared baking sheet, cheese side up.

5. Place baking sheet on upper oven rack (top quarter of oven) and bake for 4-5 minutes, or until cheese is melted and top of bread is slightly browned.

6. Remove skewers and serve mini sandwiches alongside a salad and dipping sauces.

Serve these sandwiches alongside a selection of dressings, such as our Creamy Parmesan Dressing on page 54, Pesto Mayo Dressing on page 56, or Garlic Dressing on page 62.

YIELD
3-4 servings

TIDBIT:
The baguette as we know it dates to the 1920s and is a by-product of a protective labor law that prevented French bakers from working between 10 p.m. and 4 a.m. That made it impossible for them to prepare traditional round loaves by breakfast time. Bakers had to turn to a new kind of bread, with a narrow shape that made it faster to prepare and bake.

OH, baguettes. It's so tricky to choose the right one. Make sure you buy a relatively narrow baguette that's not over-baked. Since this one will be toasted in the oven again before serving, you don't want one that's extra crispy to begin.

This recipe is not just about looks. While it's one of the prettiest sandwiches I've ever made, it's the technique that won me over. Slicing and skewering the sandwich will help you achieve more crispiness outside, while keeping the insides soft and irresistible.

—L.

Grilled Avocado Sandwich

INGREDIENTS

6	slices whole wheat bread
1	ripe avocado
1 tsp	lemon juice
⅛–¼ tsp	kosher salt
•	pinch coarse black pepper
1	plum tomato, thinly sliced
2-3	slices Muenster cheese
½ Tbsp	butter

GARLIC DRESSING:

4 Tbsp	mayonnaise
1	garlic clove, crushed
¾ tsp	lemon juice
¼ tsp	mustard
⅛ tsp	Worcestershire sauce OR soy sauce
¼ tsp	kosher salt
1 Tbsp	water

INSTRUCTIONS

1. In a small bowl, using a fork, finely mash avocado. Add lemon juice, salt, and pepper.

2. Prepare the dressing: In a small bowl, combine mayonnaise, garlic, lemon juice, mustard, Worcestershire sauce, salt, and water. Use an immersion blender to blend the mixture until smooth (you can also do this in a mini chopper).

3. Smear avocado mixture over 3 slices of bread. Layer tomato over avocado. Drizzle with dressing; top with Muenster cheese and remaining bread slices.

4. Grease a panini or waffle maker with butter (or butter the bread directly). Add sandwiches and cook until bread is golden and cheese is melted, about 3 minutes.

YIELD
3 sandwiches

To make this sandwich in a frying pan, melt butter over medium heat. Add sandwich and cook until bread is golden, about 3 minutes, pressing sandwich down as it cooks (you can also press it with a pot). Flip sandwich and cook on the other side until bread is golden and cheese is melted.

CaN everyone's favorite grilled cheese sandwich be topped? I top mine by combining warm avocado with melted cheese. This combo also works great in a fried egg roll or in our Hasselback Baguettes (page 60). −L.

Sounds amazing, but why did you write 4 Tablespoons mayo? We usually write ¼ cup. −V.

Because you can't fit a ¼-cup measuring cup in the mayo jar! It's easier to just stick in that tablespoon 4 times. Don't you all agree? −L.

Eggplant Parmesan Wraps

INGREDIENTS

EGGPLANT:

1	eggplant
2	eggs
1 cup	plain breadcrumbs
2 tsp	dried minced onion
1 tsp	garlic powder
1 tsp	Italian seasoning
¾-1 tsp	kosher salt
•	oil, for frying

FOR ASSEMBLY:

4	large wheat wraps
1	large tomato, sliced
1	onion, thinly sliced
1 cup	shredded mozzarella cheese
2 Tbsp	Parmesan cheese (optional)

INSTRUCTIONS

1. Cut eggplant into ½-inch-thick slices. Cut slices into half moons. Place eggplant slices into a colander and sprinkle with salt. Let sit for 20-30 minutes to emit bitter liquid; rinse.

2. In a shallow bowl, beat the eggs.

3. In a second shallow bowl, combine breadcrumbs, onion, garlic, Italian seasoning, and salt.

4. Dip eggplant slices into egg, then coat in breadcrumbs.

5. Heat 1 inch oil in a frying pan over medium heat. When oil is hot, add eggplant slices and fry for 2 minutes on each side. Remove to a paper towel-lined plate.

6. Preheat oven to 400°F.

7. Place wrap on work surface. Place eggplant slices across one side of wrap. Top with tomato, onion, and cheeses. Fold wrap over and press down to close. Repeat with remaining wraps. Spray tops of wraps with nonstick cooking spray or brush with oil.

8. Place wraps onto a baking sheet. Bake for 7-10 minutes, until crispy. Serve alongside warm marinara or pizza sauce.

YIELD
4 sandwiches

To bake your eggplant slices instead of frying them, brush baking sheet generously with oil and place eggplant slices in a single layer over oil. Spray eggplant with nonstick cooking spray and bake at 400°F for 25 minutes, until eggplant is golden.

Have extra sautéed vegetables? Tuck them into a wrap and make a half moon-style sandwich like this one.

CLASSIC Eggplant Parmesan has lots of delicious marinara sauce. But if you add sauce to a sandwich, the bread will soak it up and get soggy. So I leave it out of this sandwich, and serve the sauce on the side (see page 10).

—L.

Cheesy Bread

INGREDIENTS

1	(8-10 in) baguette
2 Tbsp	butter, softened
2 Tbsp	mayonnaise
1 tsp	garlic powder
¼ cup	shredded cheese (a mix of mozzarella and cheddar works well)

INSTRUCTIONS

1. Preheat oven or toaster oven to 425°F. Slice open baguette.

2. Cut butter into small bits. In a small bowl, combine butter bits, mayonnaise, and garlic. Stir in cheese. Divide spread between baguette halves.

3. Place baguette halves on baking sheet and toast for 10-12 minutes in the oven or 5 minutes in the toaster oven, until baguette is crispy at the edges.

To soften butter quickly, cut it into small pieces or roll it out between two pieces of parchment paper.

YIELD
1 sandwich

TIDBIT:
The makeup of the baguette's dough is defined by French law. The law clarifies which additives, if any, may be added and how they can be used.

Although we use the term "garlic powder," the best type of dried ground garlic to stock in your spice cabinet is called "granulated garlic."

ONE day, while Victoria and I were both testing recipes, Victoria sent me a photo of her lunch: the Peach Cobbler Smoothie from page 24. Then, I sent her back a photo of my lunch: this Cheesy Bread. The most awesome baguette I ever had. I think I won Best Lunch that day. —L.

MAKE IT!

Chocolate Pizza

YES, we can have pizza for dessert too. To make the chocolate ganache, melt 2 ounces chocolate and whisk in a ¼ cup heavy cream. Spread over one pizza dough (either our Bistro-Style Pizza Dough on page 70 or Thin-Crust Pizza Dough on page 72 will work). Scatter marshmallows on top and sprinkle with a mixture of cinnamon and confectioners' sugar. Bake as directed and drizzle with dulce de leche.

Pizza

Bistro-Style Pizza Dough

INGREDIENTS

2½ cups	warm water
1 oz	fresh yeast OR 3¼ tsp dry yeast
1 Tbsp	sugar
6¾-7 cups	flour
4 Tbsp	olive oil
1 Tbsp	salt

FOR ASSEMBLING EACH PIZZA:

•	cornmeal, for sprinkling
5-6 Tbsp	pizza sauce (see page 10)
¾ cup	shredded mozzarella cheese

Don't have a pizza stone? Use a heavy baking sheet, which will also retain heat and help your pizza get crispy.

INSTRUCTIONS

1. In the bowl of an electric mixer, combine water and yeast. Add sugar, 6½ cups flour, olive oil, and salt; knead until a smooth dough forms. Gradually add in remaining flour, if necessary, until dough feels just a little sticky.

2. Place dough into a greased bowl; turn the dough over in the bowl so it is greased all around. Cover with a clean towel or plastic wrap; let rise at least 3 hours (or up to 4-5 hours).

3. Preheat oven to 450°F. Divide dough into four balls and let rest for 3-4 minutes.

4. On a floured surface, press dough ball into a 12-inch circle. Sprinkle a piece of parchment paper with cornmeal and place the dough onto it.

5. Top with sauce. Trim edges of parchment paper to about 2 inches beyond the edge of the pizza.

6. **If baking using a pizza stone:** Make sure your pizza stone has preheated for a minimum of 30 minutes. Place pizza with parchment on stone and bake for 5 minutes. **If baking using a heavy baking sheet:** Place pizza with parchment on baking sheet and bake for 6-7 minutes.

7. Remove pizza from oven. Top with cheese and/or toppings. Return to oven; bake for additional 5-7 minutes.

YIELD
4 (12-inch) pizzas
(or 4 balls of dough)

Why cornmeal? White or yellow cornmeal complements pizza dough well and adds both great taste and correct texture.

For a dark, crispy top, you can broil your pizza for a few seconds — but watch it carefully!

THE reason it's hard to recreate perfect bistro-style pizza at home is because most of us don't have brick or wood-fired ovens. Another reason is that we don't use the same flour. Italian pizza is usually made using a type called 00 flour (a highly refined and finely ground flour), which is not widely available. We didn't let that stop us!   —L.

30-Minute Thin-Crust Pizza Dough

INGREDIENTS

1½ cups	warm water
2¼ tsp	dry yeast
1 tsp	sugar
4 cups	flour
2½ tsp	salt
1½ Tbsp	cornmeal

INSTRUCTIONS

1. Prepare the dough: In a large bowl or the bowl of an electric mixer, combine water, yeast, and sugar. Stir in flour and then salt. Knead until dough comes together. Dough will be a bit sticky. Place dough into a greased bowl; turn the dough over in the bowl so it is greased all around. Cover with a clean towel or plastic wrap; let rise 30-40 minutes.

2. Preheat oven to 475°F. Divide dough into 2 balls. Sprinkle two pieces of parchment paper with cornmeal. Place each dough ball onto parchment paper. Using a floured rolling pin, roll each dough ball into a 14-inch circle with ¼-inch thickness. Transfer parchment paper with dough to a baking sheet.

3. Top with desired toppings. Bake until crust is golden and crispy on the bottom, 12-13 minutes.

Since this dough will make two pies, you can make two different versions of thin-crust pizzas (try both of our favorite toppings on the following pages), or turn the second pie into a classic sauce-and-cheese version for the kids.

YIELD

2 (14-inch) pizzas
(or 2 balls of dough)

INSPIRED BY COOKKOSHER MEMBER
Dassie

TIDBIT:

For 50 years, the price of a pizza slice has matched, with uncanny precision, the cost of a NYC subway ride. Economists have named it "The Pizza Principle."

This dough can also be used to make a crispy French bread. Shape into loaves and bake for 20-25 minutes.

SO many great pizza dough recipes need time. And time isn't always on our side. This dough was originally used to make a French bread, but it's perfect as a thin and crispy pizza dough. A thin dough works great when you want to highlight flavorful pizza toppings (I like it with the Honey Pomodoro Topping on the following page) ... or when you simply don't have much time.   —V.

Honey Pomodoro Pizza

INGREDIENTS

2 Tbsp	olive oil
1	onion, cut into thin strips
2 pints	grape tomatoes, halved
3	garlic cloves, crushed
2 Tbsp	honey
2 Tbsp	vinegar
1 Tbsp	Dijon mustard
1 tsp	salt
•	pinch coarse black pepper
1	ball pizza dough (see Bistro-Style Pizza Dough, page 70, or Thin-Crust Pizza Dough, page 72)
½ lb	fresh mozzarella cheese, cut into rounds

INSTRUCTIONS

1. Heat oil in a sauté pan over medium-low heat. Add onions and sauté until golden, about 10 minutes. Add tomatoes and garlic; sauté an additional 5 minutes. Stir in honey, vinegar, mustard, salt, and pepper. Cook an additional 1-2 minutes.

2. Roll pizza dough into a thin 14-inch circle. Spread topping over pizza dough. Top with mozzarella rounds. Bake as directed on page 70 or 72.

Fresh mozzarella, such as Natural & Kosher's, is always better on top of a gourmet-style pizza. We also love it on top of our Roasted Veggie Galette (page 36) and inside our Frittata (page 14).

YIELD
2 pies

TIDBIT:
The largest pizza ever recorded measured 122 feet 8 inches in diameter, weighed 26,883 pounds, and contained 9,920 pounds of flour, 3,960 pounds of cheese, 1,763 pounds of mushrooms, 1,984 pounds of tomato puree, and 1,984 pounds of chopped tomatoes.

We like this topping best over a thin crust pizza.

I was very skeptical when my sister-in-law Rachel said that this is her family's favorite pizza topping. But now, I'm totally sold. These days, when I make pizza for dinner, I prepare a classic pie for the kids while the adults savor this one. I named this pizza "Pomodoro," which means "tomato" in Italian.   —V.

Pizza Bianca

INGREDIENTS

3-4 Tbsp	oil
1	onion, cut into thin strips
2 Tbsp	butter
2 Tbsp	flour
2 cups	milk
1 tsp	salt
1 ball	pizza dough (see Bistro-Style Pizza Dough on page 70 or Thin-Crust Pizza Dough on page 72)
¾ cup	shredded mozzarella cheese
2 tsp	minced fresh basil
1 Tbsp	grated Parmesan cheese

INSTRUCTIONS

1. Heat oil in a sauté pan over medium heat. Add onion and sauté until golden, 10-12 minutes. Set aside.

2. Meanwhile, prepare the Bianca sauce: Melt butter in a second sauté pan over medium heat. Whisk in flour. Gradually add in milk, whisking to combine. Raise heat and bring to a boil. Lower heat and simmer, stirring constantly, until sauce thickens, about 10 minutes. Remove from heat and season with salt.

3. Press pizza dough into a 12-inch circle and top with Bianca sauce, onions, mozzarella, basil, and Parmesan cheese. Bake as directed on page 70 or 72.

Don't try to double this sauce. A larger recipe will take too long to thicken and the milk may scald.

YIELD
1 pizza

TIDBIT:
The reason it is so tough to replicate NYC pizza has to do with the taste of the water in New York. Nearly every chemical reaction that produces flavor occurs in water and with different water a very different taste results.

"Bianca" is the Italian word for "white."

Is it possible for there to be a sauce that ... could it be ... rivals classic tomato-based pizza sauce? Yes: This buttery, heavenly white sauce. Make sure some makes it onto your pizza. —L.

Israeli Pizza Dip

INGREDIENTS

½ cup	mayonnaise
½ cup	tomato sauce
½	Israeli pickle
½ tsp	yellow mustard
½ tsp	paprika
¼ tsp	onion powder
¼ tsp	garlic powder
¼ tsp	dried basil
¼ tsp	dried oregano
¼ tsp	cayenne pepper
¼ tsp	crushed red pepper flakes, or more to taste
¼ tsp	kosher salt
⅛ tsp	coarse black pepper

Israeli pickles are made from small gherkins and are pickled in salt water only. In the US, they are usually sold in a can.

INSTRUCTIONS

- In the bowl of a mini chopper, combine mayonnaise, tomato sauce, pickle, mustard, and spices. Blend until smooth.

YIELD 1 cup

AMERICANS may be known for having the best kosher pizza shops, but it's the Israelis who perfected the perfect sauce for dipping the pizza. How to eat this? Drizzle it over your ready pizza or place it into a small bowl and dip the pizza into it. Don't neglect your French fries! This also beats ketchup.   –L.

Want to get your pizza dip to be the same consistency as the pizza shops do? Most pizza shops will use less-expensive brands of mayo when preparing their dip. So save your premium mayo for your salad dressing and use another brand for your dips.

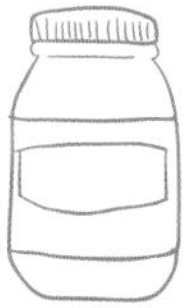

Herbed Pull-Apart Bread

INGREDIENTS

5 Tbsp	oil
¼ cup	shredded cheese
2	scallions, sliced
1 tsp	dried basil
1 tsp	garlic powder
1 ball	pizza dough (see Bistro-Style Pizza Dough on page 70, or Thin-Crust Pizza Dough on page 72)

INSTRUCTIONS

1. Preheat oven to 425°F. Grease a 6-cup muffin pan.

2. In a small bowl, combine oil, cheese, scallions, basil, and garlic.

3. Divide dough into 18-24 balls. Roll each ball in the cheese mixture. Pile 3-4 balls into each muffin cup. Let rise 15-20 minutes.

4. Bake until golden, 18-20 minutes.

YIELD 6 portions

THESE little buns make the perfect appetizer. Serve them with a dipping bowl of pizza sauce on the side and pull away.   −L.

Caramelized Onion Calzones

INGREDIENTS

1 Tbsp	butter
1 Tbsp	oil
2	medium red onions, thinly sliced
1 tsp	brown sugar
¼ tsp	salt
1 tsp	balsamic vinegar
2 Tbsp	(heaping) cream cheese
½ cup	shredded cheese
1	ball pizza dough (see Bistro-Style Pizza Dough on page 70 or Thin-Crust Pizza Dough on page 72)
1	egg, lightly beaten
•	sesame seeds, for sprinkling

INSTRUCTIONS

1. Preheat oven to 425°F. Line a baking sheet with parchment paper.

2. Melt butter with oil in a skillet over medium-low heat. Add onions, brown sugar, and salt; sauté until golden, about 20 minutes. Add balsamic vinegar and continue to cook until onions are caramelized, about 5 additional minutes.

3. Divide dough in half. Roll each half into an 8-inch square and place with corner facing you. Spread 1 tablespoon cream cheese vertically down the center of each square. Top each square with half the onion mixture and half the shredded cheese.

4. Fold each corner horizontally over the filling. Brush with egg and sprinkle with sesame seeds. Place calzones on prepared baking sheet and bake for 15 minutes, until golden.

YIELD
2 large calzones

TIDBIT:
350 slices of pizza are sold every second in America. That doesn't include calzones.

ONE afternoon, I set out to discover the best calzone filling. I visited all the local pizza shops and asked, "What's your most popular calzone?" Then I went home and made all the different types ... including this version that I didn't see in any pizza shop.

Since there were too many for me to eat, I sent them out with a neighbor who was on her way to work. Ten minutes later, her co-workers requested more of the caramelized onion version. My café was closed. Here's the recipe. Make your own!   –L.

MAKE IT!

1-2-3 Sauce

WANT to fake a great pasta dinner? Here's the quickie way to great sauce.

PENNE À LA VODKA: Combine 1 (26-oz) jar Marinara-style Vodka Sauce and 2 cups heavy cream in a saucepan over medium heat. When heated through, add 3 tablespoons Parmesan cheese.

PESTO CREAM SAUCE. Combine 1-2 tablespoons oil and ½ cup prepared pesto in a saucepan over medium heat. Add 2 cups heavy cream. Raise heat and bring to a boil. Add 3 tablespoons Parmesan cheese and salt and pepper to taste.

ALFREDO SAUCE: Melt 2 tablespoons butter. Add 2 tablespoons flour; stir. Add 2 cups heavy cream; bring to a boil. Lower heat and add about ½ cup Parmesan cheese. Cook until thickened.

Pasta

Cannelloni *with* Milk Sauce

INGREDIENTS

3 cups	marinara or pizza sauce
1 lb	manicotti tubes

FILLING:

1 cup	ricotta cheese
16-oz	frozen spinach, thawed and completely drained
½ cup	grated Parmesan cheese
1	egg
½ tsp	kosher salt
•	pinch coarse black pepper

MILK SAUCE:

¼ cup	(½ stick) butter
½ cup	flour
2½ cups	milk

INSTRUCTIONS

1. Preheat oven to 350°F. Grease a 9 x 13-inch ovenproof dish. Pour marinara sauce into the prepared dish.

2. Prepare the filling: In a medium bowl, combine ricotta cheese, spinach, Parmesan cheese, egg, salt, and pepper. Place the filling into a piping bag or resealable plastic bag and snip off the corner. Pipe filling into raw manicotti tubes. Line tubes over sauce in prepared dish. For a prettier presentation, allow some space between the tubes.

3. Prepare the milk sauce: Melt butter in a medium saucepan over low heat. Stir in flour. Gradually add milk, a little at a time, whisking as you pour to dissolve the flour. Cook until sauce thickens, about 10 minutes.

4. Pour sauce over tubes and bake for 50-60 minutes, until pasta tubes are soft and top of sauce becomes lightly golden.

YIELD

14 tubes

INSPIRED BY COOKKOSHER MEMBER

Doctor

Both cannelloni and manicotti are made using the same pasta tubes. Manicotti refers to a dish that uses a tomato-based sauce on top, while cannelloni features a white sauce on top.

For a kid-friendly version, replace spinach with 1 additional cup ricotta cheese.

STUFFeD shells used to be the dish I'd make when filling my freezer with ready-to-go dinners for busy nights. Though it always pleased the whole family, the process of boiling and stuffing those shells didn't please mommy so much. Stuffed cannelloni is way easier (no boiling required! No awkward messy filling process!) and the irresistible milk sauce on top makes it taste much better too. These disappear quicker than stuffed shells ever did.   —V.

Sweet Potato Pasta

INGREDIENTS

1 lb	spaghetti or penne
2	sweet potatoes, peeled and diced
2 Tbsp	butter
2 tsp	flour
2 cups	milk
½ cup	heavy cream
1 cup	shredded mozzarella cheese
1 tsp	kosher salt

INSTRUCTIONS

1. Prepare pasta according to package directions.

2. Meanwhile, add potatoes to a medium saucepan. Cover with water and bring to a boil. Boil until soft, about 20 minutes. Drain and mash.

3. Melt butter in a sauté pan over medium heat. Whisk in flour. Slowly add milk and heavy cream and whisk until smooth. Bring to a simmer and cook until sauce thickens.

4. Gradually add mashed sweet potatoes, whisking until smooth. Cook for an additional 5 minutes.

5. Add pasta, a little bit at a time, to the sauce. Add in cheese and mix until melted. Season with salt. Serve hot.

YIELD
8 servings

INSPIRED BY COOKKOSHER MEMBER

frosting

Serving family members with more sophisticated taste buds? Fresh or dried thyme is a great pairing with this pasta.

For a garnish like this, you'll need to use a cheese grater to shave pieces from Natural & Kosher's whole Parmesan cheese.

SOMETIMES parents are tired of eating kid-friendly pasta. We want to experience more flavors. But who wants to prepare two different dinners? Then, here comes this sweet potato pasta, with surprising flavor to make the adults happy, but with a creaminess that kept my kids thrilled too (plus it's a kid-friendly color).

And though it tastes extremely rich, the sauce is made with mostly milk and only a bit of cream. After all the tons of pasta we've been testing and eating while writing this book, this is the one I dream about the most. —V.

Cajun Creamy Penne

INGREDIENTS

¾ lb	penne
2 Tbsp	butter
2	plum tomatoes, diced
¼ tsp	paprika
¼ tsp	chili powder
½ tsp	cayenne pepper
½ tsp	garlic powder
2	scallions, diced
1¾ cups	heavy cream
½ tsp	kosher salt
¼ tsp	coarse black pepper

INSTRUCTIONS

1. Prepare pasta according to package directions.

2. Meanwhile, prepare the sauce: Melt butter in a sauté pan over medium heat. Add tomatoes and sauté over high heat for 4-5 minutes. Add paprika, chili powder, cayenne pepper, and garlic powder. Add scallions and heavy cream; cook an additional 3-4 minutes.

3. Add pasta to cream, a little at a time, and toss to coat. Season with salt and pepper.

YIELD
4 servings

Surprisingly, some commentators state that at times when the Torah refers to chalav, it doesn't mean milk at all. Rather, the verse is referring to white wine.

Not all shapes are created equal. Some smaller pasta shapes with more surface area, like elbows or rotini, will need a bit more sauce.

IF you like alfredo sauce on your pasta and enjoy a little kick, like I do, this pasta is for you.

—L.

Calsones

INGREDIENTS

- **8 oz**   shredded Muenster cheese
- **2**   eggs
- **•**   pinch baking powder
- **1**   (36-pk) ravioli dough rounds, thawed
- **1 lb**   broad egg noodles
- **¼ cup**   (½ stick) butter
- **1 tsp**   kosher salt

If frozen ravioli dough isn't sold in your neighborhood, you can use wonton wrappers. Lightly wet the edges when sealing closed.

INSTRUCTIONS

1. In a small bowl, combine cheese, eggs, and baking powder. The cheese should look wet.

2. Line a baking sheet with parchment paper. Place ravioli rounds on baking sheet (you won't be able to fit all of them at first, but you will as you go along). Don't leave ravioli dough exposed to air when not in use or they will dry out.

3. Place a heaping teaspoon of cheese in the center of each ravioli round. Fold dough over; seal closed in a half moon shape, then pinch the 2 ends of the dough together. Freeze raviolis until ready to use.

4. When ready to cook, preheat oven to 350°F. Bring a large stockpot of water to boil. Add frozen raviolis and boil for 10 minutes. Add egg noodles and boil an additional 10 minutes. Drain and return all to the pot. Stir in butter and salt.

5. Pour pasta into an ovenproof casserole dish and bake until pasta is golden on top, about 60 minutes. (You can omit this step or bake for minimal time if you find you like it soft rather than crispy, or bake longer for extra crispiness.)

YIELD

8 servings

Calsones is easy to prepare ahead. You can freeze big batches of filled raviolis and boil as needed. Or, freeze or refrigerate the whole prepared casserole, whether or not it is baked. Simply bake until hot before serving (keep it uncovered for crispy pasta or covered to keep it softer).

Don't confuse calsones with calzones! Calsones is pronounced kal·so´·nes.

BACK in *Starters & Sides Made Easy*, I told you that while I love making fresh dough, when it comes to ravioli, the frozen work just fine for me. And that's what I use when I make calsones. If there ever was a traditional Syrian dish whose time has come to break into the world, calsones is it. The ingredients are super basic, and it even works well as a make-ahead dish. Whether you like yours on the soft side (like my husband's side of the family), or the authentic way, super brown and crunchy (like my side of the family), you'll adopt this pasta dish as your own tradition.   —V.

Avocado *and* Basil Pasta Salad

INGREDIENTS

8 oz	bow-tie pasta or macaroni
2	medium avocados, diced
⅔ cup	loosely packed basil leaves, chopped OR ¼ cup chopped fresh or frozen basil
2 Tbsp	freshly squeezed lemon juice
1 Tbsp	olive oil
3	garlic cloves, crushed
¼ tsp	kosher salt
•	pinch coarse black pepper
½ cup	grated Parmesan cheese

INSTRUCTIONS

1. Prepare pasta according to package directions.
2. Meanwhile, in a large bowl, combine avocado, basil, lemon juice, olive oil, garlic, salt, and pepper.
3. Add hot pasta to bowl; stir to combine. Sprinkle with Parmesan cheese and serve at room temperature.

YIELD
4 servings

INSPIRED BY COOKKOSHER MEMBER
ngolovin

To assemble this quickly when company is coming, combine basil, lemon juice, olive oil, garlic, salt, and pepper in advance to create a dressing. Boil pasta and toss with dressing, avocado, and Parmesan.

REMEMBER those tri-color pasta salads with heavy mayo dressings? I never liked those. I used to think there was no way to serve room temperature pasta that I liked as much as I like my creamy hot pastas. Well, now we found one. -L.

Baked Roasted Veggie Pasta

INGREDIENTS

1 lb	fusilli or penne pasta
2 pints	cherry tomatoes, halved
2	red onions, cut into wedges
1	zucchini, cut into half moons
¼ cup	olive oil
½ tsp	garlic powder
•	kosher salt, to taste
•	coarse black pepper, to taste
6 oz	feta cheese, crumbled
1 Tbsp	chopped fresh or frozen basil

INSTRUCTIONS

1. Prepare pasta according to package directions.

2. Preheat oven to 400°F. In a 9 x 13-inch pan, combine cherry tomatoes, red onions, and zucchini. Toss with olive oil and garlic powder. Bake for 30 minutes, stirring occasionally.

3. Add pasta to vegetables and mix well. Season with salt and pepper.

4. Preheat oven to broil and broil for 10 minutes, stirring after 5 minutes.

5. Add feta cheese and basil; stir to combine (the heat will melt the cheese). Serve hot or at room temperature.

YIELD
8 servings

You can add more veggies to the mix. We also love this pasta with red peppers instead of tomatoes.

We made the pasta In this photo using broken lasagna sheets.

THE evolution of this recipe goes something like this. Devorah, my sister-in-law, has been making roasted vegetables, tossing them with prepared pasta, and broiling the dish to attain some crispy bits. It's become her staple for shalosh seudos and brunches. Then, her sister-in-law Tzippy began preparing Devorah's pasta with one difference ... she added feta cheese. Baam! Now an awesome pasta was even better.

–L.

Classic Spaghetti *with* Buttery Tomato Sauce

INGREDIENTS

1 lb	spaghetti or linguine
5 Tbsp	butter, divided
2	garlic cloves, crushed
2 cups	fresh diced tomatoes
1 tsp	kosher salt
1	(15-oz) can tomato sauce
•	pinch sugar
•	Parmesan cheese, for sprinkling (optional)

INSTRUCTIONS

1. Prepare pasta according to package instructions.

2. Melt 4 tablespoons butter in a sauté pan over medium heat. Add garlic and cook for 1 minute. Add tomatoes and salt; sauté for 3-4 minutes. Add tomato sauce and sugar; cook for 10 minutes. Stir in remaining 1 tablespoon butter.

3. Pour sauce over pasta. Sprinkle with Parmesan cheese, if desired, and serve.

YIELD
6 servings

You can blend the sauce for a smooth consistency.

I'M sometimes amazed at the creativity of chefs when I look at the menus at dairy restaurants (cashews + caramelized onions?). But the classics are always on the menu. And for good reason! Don't mess with the best!

—L.

MAKE IT!

Chocolate Chip Cookie Desserts

OUR dairy cookies deserve some ice cream.

To make the chocolate chip cookie ice cream sandwiches, add a scoop of ice cream to a cookie and top with another cookie. Press into a sandwich, roll in melted chocolate, and freeze until set.

To make chocolate chip cookies à la mode, warm the cookies. Top with ice cream, whipped cream, and berries. Serve with a dash of chocolate sauce.

Desserts

Cheese Buns

INGREDIENTS

DOUGH:

¾ cup	warm milk
4 tsp	instant dry yeast
½ cup	sugar
6 cups	flour
½ tsp	kosher salt
¼ cup	orange juice
1 tsp	vanilla extract
1¼ cup	(2½ sticks) butter, at room temperature
2	eggs
2	egg yolks

FILLING:

1½	(8-oz) containers whipped cream cheese
¾ cup	confectioners' sugar
1	egg yolk
1½ tsp	vanilla extract
1½	(3.5 oz) bars white chocolate

INSTRUCTIONS

1. In the bowl of an electric mixer, combine warm milk, yeast, and sugar. Add flour, salt, orange juice, vanilla, butter, eggs, and yolks. Knead until smooth. Let dough rest 1 hour. It will not rise much.

2. Prepare the filling: In a large bowl, combine cream cheese, confectioners' sugar, egg yolk, and vanilla.

3. Melt white chocolate over a double boiler. Immediately add to cream cheese mixture and stir until smooth.

4. Prepare the streusel: In a medium bowl, combine butter, sugar, vanilla, and flour. Using your fingers, mix together until crumbs form.

5. Divide dough into thirds. One at a time, roll each piece into a 10 x 17-inch rectangle. Smear ⅓ of the filling over each rectangle. Roll up, jelly-roll style. Pull back as you roll to ensure the rolls are tight and narrow.

6. Slice each roll into 12 pieces. Place each piece into a mini cheesecake or muffin pan. Brush with melted butter and sprinkle with streusel. Bake for 20 minutes. Let cool; dust with confectioners' sugar.

YIELD
36 buns

To bake your cheese buns so they rise tall like these, you'll need a mini cheesecake pan with removable bottom, such as Norpro's.

For a cheese babka, bake one of your rolls in a loaf pan.

WHILE we were working on this book, a neighbor came over and said, "You're writing a dairy cookbook? I want a cheese version of this in the book." She took out her phone and showed me a photo of a cinnamon bun. The beautiful bun was the work of Kiki Fischer. I tracked down Kiki, demanded her bun-creating secrets, then created this dairy buttery version. Yes, it is the most complicated recipe in this book. Most people would not call this easy. But I think the photo tells you why we absolutely had to listen to my neighbor's request. —L.

STREUSEL:

¼ cup	(½ stick) **butter**, at room temperature
¼ cup	sugar
½ tsp	vanilla extract
¾ cup	flour

FOR ASSEMBLY:

| 2 Tbsp | **butter**, melted |
| • | **confectioners' sugar**, for dusting |

Daskal's Cheesecake

INGREDIENTS

CRUST:

2 cups	crushed chocolate chip cookies
2 Tbsp	butter, melted

CREAM CHEESE BATTER:

1½ lb	brick-style cream cheese
1 cup	sugar
3 Tbsp	flour
1 Tbsp	vanilla sugar
4	eggs
5 oz	sour cream
6 oz	heavy cream
1 tsp	coffee diluted in 1 Tbsp water

GANACHE TOPPING:

1	(3.5-oz) Rosemarie chocolate bar
3 tsp	corn syrup
1 tsp	coffee diluted in 2 Tbsp water

INSTRUCTIONS

1. Preheat oven to 350°F. Line a 10-inch springform pan with parchment paper.

2. In a small bowl, combine crushed cookies and butter. Press into prepared pan.

3. In the bowl of an electric mixer, beat cream cheese with sugar until smooth. Add in flour, vanilla, and eggs, one at a time.

4. Whisk together sour cream, heavy cream, and coffee mixture. Add to mixer bowl and mix until just combined. Pour batter over crust.

5. Bake on lower rack of oven for 1 hour. Let cool; refrigerate overnight before serving.

6. When cake is cool, prepare the ganache: Melt the chocolate and whisk in corn syrup and coffee mixture. Spread over cooled cake.

YIELD

1 (10-inch) round cake

Chanie recommends using soft cream cheese, which is only sold in 5-pound containers. Ask your grocer to order a container for you if you'll be making a few cheesecakes.

We had a really hard time figuring out what kind of cheesecake recipe we wanted to include in this book. Should we share a classic cheesecake or something new and different? Everyone has a cheesecake they make and love. What would make ours better? Well, a cheesecake is definitely the best if it comes from Chanie Daskal, the baker behind Daskal's Delights. She is renowned for her creamy cheesecakes and dairy desserts. When Chanie shared this recipe with us, we knew this was the one. An awesome cheesecake from the cheesecake queen. —L.

THE 180 Cal (or less!) Cheesecake

INGREDIENTS

- 2 (6-oz) containers plain Greek yogurt
- ½ cup sugar OR sugar substitute
- 2 eggs
- 2 tsp vanilla extract
- ⅛ tsp kosher salt
- 1 Tbsp cornstarch
- 1 graham cracker pie crust

You can make flavored cheesecakes using any of Norman's Greek yogurt varieties, such as Lite Strawberry or Coffee.

INSTRUCTIONS

1. Preheat oven to 350°F.

2. In a blender, combine yogurt, sugar, eggs, vanilla, salt, and cornstarch. Blend to combine (you can also use an immersion blender). Pour into crust.

3. Bake for 30 minutes or until cake is beginning to turn golden on top. It will seem slightly jiggly, but will continue to set as it cools.

4. Refrigerate for at least 6 hours before serving.

YIELD
8 servings

INSPIRED BY COOKKOSHER MEMBER
malkie

To make your cheesecakes in advance, cover and keep refrigerated for up to 1 week. You can also freeze and thaw at room temperature.

IT'S 40 calories per slice if you bake it in ramekins (without a crust) and use a sugar substitute. It's 80 calories with real sugar. It's 140 calories with a sugar substitute and a graham cracker crust. Or 180 calories with both sugar and the crust. Either way, while other lower-calories cheesecakes are still loaded in calories, this is the first truly low-cal cheesecake. Cut yourself a slice, sit down, and enjoy it. But, remember, it's not low cal if you eat the whole thing!

–V.

Chocolate Cheese Muffin *with* Chocolate Ganache

INGREDIENTS

1 cup	flour
½ cup	cocoa
1 tsp	baking powder
•	pinch kosher salt
6 Tbsp	butter
1 cup	sugar
1	egg
•	scant ¾ cup milk

FILLING:

12 oz	(1½ containers) whipped cream cheese
4 tsp	vanilla extract
½ cup	sugar
½ cup	mini chocolate chips

GANACHE:

4 oz	bittersweet chocolate, chopped OR ¾ cup chocolate chips
½ cup	heavy cream

INSTRUCTIONS

1. Preheat oven to 350°F. Line a muffin pan with cupcake liners.

2. In a large bowl, sift together flour, cocoa, baking powder, and salt.

3. In the bowl of an electric mixer, combine butter and sugar. Beat at medium speed for at least 1 minute. Add egg and beat until combined. At low speed, gradually add half the flour mixture, then milk, then remaining flour mixture. Beat until combined.

4. Prepare the filling: Whisk together cream cheese, vanilla, sugar, and chocolate chips (this can be done either by hand or using a mixer).

5. Pour a small amount of chocolate batter into each cupcake liner (just enough to cover the bottom). Add a heaping teaspoon of cheese filling. Cover with additional chocolate batter until cupcake liner is two-thirds full. Bake for 20 minutes. Let cool.

6. Prepare the ganache: Combine chocolate and heavy cream in a double boiler. Heat, stirring occasionally, until chocolate is melted. Stir to combine. Remove from heat.

7. When muffins are cool, dip tops in ganache. Refrigerate until set.

YIELD
14 muffins

When used in a recipe, "scant" means "just short" or "a teensy bit less."

To make ganache in the microwave, melt chocolate and whisk in cream while chocolate is hot. We topped these with Klik's chocolate candies.

We can't have a dairy cookbook without an amazing cheese muffin. So I baked lots of them until my cousin Yitty, who loves dairy cakes, told me about this one. We have a winner.   –L.

Peach *and* Streusel Napoleon

INGREDIENTS

16	round wonton wrappers
2 Tbsp	butter, melted
•	pinch kosher salt
1 tsp	brown sugar

STREUSEL:

¼ cup	(½ stick) cold butter
2 Tbsp	brown sugar
1 Tbsp	sugar
4-5 Tbsp	flour

PEACHES:

1 Tbsp	butter
2 Tbsp	sugar
4	peaches, sliced

> No need to peel the peaches. When peaches aren't in season, use frozen.

INSTRUCTIONS

1. Preheat oven to 350°F. Line a baking sheet with parchment paper.

2. Place wonton wrappers on prepared baking sheet. In a small bowl, combine butter, salt, and brown sugar. Brush onto wonton wrappers. Bake for 4-5 minutes. Watch wrappers carefully so they don't burn.

3. Prepare the streusel: Line a baking sheet with parchment paper. In a small bowl, combine butter, sugars, and flour. Using your fingers, mix together to form into coarse crumbs. Spread on prepared baking sheet, and bake until browned, 10-12 minutes. Let cool and break crumbs apart.

4. Prepare the peaches: In a small saucepan, melt butter with sugar. Add peaches and cook for 4-5 minutes. Remove from heat.

5. To assemble, layer a wonton wrapper, fruit, streusel, and an additional layer of wrapper, fruit, and streusel.

YIELD
8 Napoleons

> You can prepare all the components of this dessert in advance. Store them separately. Then, just warm the peaches and assemble when you're ready to serve.

If your streusel crumbs melt together when they bake, no problem! Simply let cool and crumble.

THIS recipe will remind you why desserts are so much better with butter. And what we're missing out on when we're making parve desserts. It's amazing how such a simple ingredient can make something outstanding. This is one of my favorite desserts in the book. —L.

Peanut Butter Crème Brûlée

INGREDIENTS

6	egg yolks
6 Tbsp	sugar, plus more for sprinkling
1 quart	heavy cream
1 tsp	vanilla extract
6 Tbsp	creamy peanut butter

INSTRUCTIONS

1. Preheat oven to 325°F.

2. In a medium bowl, whisk together egg yolks and sugar until egg yolks lighten in color a bit.

3. In a medium saucepan, bring the cream and vanilla barely to a simmer. Remove from heat.

4. Place the peanut butter into a medium bowl. Whisk in 1 cup of the cream, so the peanut butter is liquified and easy to pour.

5. Whisk remaining cream, a little bit at a time, into the egg mixture. Add peanut butter mixture and whisk to combine.

6. Fill a baking pan with about ½-1 inch hot water (the water should come halfway up the sides of the ramekins when you place them into the pan). Place ramekins into the water bath. Divide batter between ramekins. Bake for 40-45 minutes. Let cool. Crème brûlée can be prepared up to a week ahead and refrigerated at this point.

7. Sprinkle tops of crème brûlées with sugar. Use a kitchen torch to melt the sugar.

YIELD
18 ramekins

It's worthwhile to invest in a whisk! A big, wide whisk will do the best job.

CRÈME brûlée is always on my dairy menu. Not only because I love to serve it, but also because I want to eat it too. Besides being one of my favorite desserts, it's quick and easy to prepare. Definitely easier than cookies. And much more impressive.

For years, before I invested in a kitchen torch, I prepared the dessert without its signature crackled top. So don't let the lack of a torch prevent you from beginning to prepare and enjoy crème brûlée. Nowadays, I have lots of fun torching these guys.   –V.

Tres Leches Cake

INGREDIENTS

Cake:

3 cups	flour
2 cups	sugar
4 tsp	baking powder
•	pinch kosher salt
10 Tbsp	(1¼ sticks) butter, cut into small bits
1¼ cups	milk
1½ tsp	vanilla extract
3	eggs

THREE MILKS:

1	(10.5-oz) container sweetened condensed milk or cream
1½ cups	whole milk
½ cup	heavy cream

FROSTING:

2 cups	heavy cream
¼ cup	sugar

INSTRUCTIONS

1. Preheat oven to 350°F. Grease bottom and sides of a 10-inch springform pan.

2. In the bowl of an electric mixer, place the flour, sugar, baking powder, and salt. Stir briefly to combine. With the mixer on low, add in butter, a little at a time.

3. In a small bowl, whisk together milk, vanilla, and eggs. Slowly add to flour mixture and beat until combined. Pour batter into prepared pan and bake for 50-60 minutes, until golden on top and center is springy to the touch. Let cool.

4. Prepare the three-milk mixture: Whisk together sweetened condensed milk, milk, and cream. Using a skewer, poke holes over the surface of the cooled cake. Pour mixture over cake. Cover and refrigerate for at least 6 hours or overnight. Cake may be frozen at this point.

5. Prepare the frosting: In the bowl of an electric mixer, combine cream and sugar. Whip until stiff. Using an offset spatula, spread over top of cake.

YIELD
12 servings

This cake will freeze well, even with the "three milks." Let thaw before frosting.

Use the base of the Tres Leches Cake whenever you're looking for a perfect fluffy sponge cake or white cake. No egg separating required!

WHILe writing this book, on most days, I subsisted on just yogurt or veggies so I could afford to experiment and taste all our cheesy recipes later in the day. I had the balancing down to a science. Until it came to this Tres Leches Cake. Tres Leches Cake for dinner. Tres Leches Cake for breakfast. And the next night, while half my family had chicken for dinner, the other half of us chose to finish the ... Tres Leches Cake. No regrets. Time to bake another cake.   —V.

Sour Cream Chocolate Chip Cake

INGREDIENTS

BATTER:

1 cup	sour cream
1 tsp	baking soda
½ cup	(1 stick) butter
1 cup	sugar
2	eggs
1 tsp	vanilla extract
1 tsp	almond extract
2 cups	flour
1 tsp	baking powder

CHOCOLATE-NUT MIXTURE:

1	(10-oz) bag chocolate chips
2 cups	coarsely chopped walnuts
1 tsp	cinnamon
¼ cup	sugar

INSTRUCTIONS

1. Preheat oven to 350°F. Grease a 10-inch tube pan.

2. In a medium bowl, combine sour cream and baking soda. Sour cream should bubble and expand. Set aside.

3. In the bowl of an electric mixer, combine butter and sugar. Beat until light and creamy. Add eggs and extracts.

4. Add half the flour and baking powder. Add sour cream mixture, then remaining flour. Beat until just combined. Do not overmix.

5. In a medium bowl, combine chocolate chips, walnuts, cinnamon, and sugar. Sprinkle some of the chocolate nut mixture into the pan. Add half the batter over it, then half of the remaining chocolate-nut mixture. Add remaining batter and top cake with remaining chocolate-nut mixture. Bake for 50-60 minutes, until top is firm and crispy. Let cool for 10 minutes before removing from pan.

YIELD
12 servings

Baking soda reacts when it comes in contact with an acid, such as sour cream. Without an acidic ingredient in a batter, unactivated baking soda will leave a soapy taste (ever wonder why a cake doesn't work when you substitute the dairy products with parve alternatives?)

You can also make this in a Bundt pan. You'll miss the crunchy top (it's still delicious on the bottom!), but you'll have pretty sides.

AT one melavah malkah where we enjoyed lots of dairy desserts, my friend Giordana Shalom and I were discussing the wonders of butter. Often, parve desserts just can't compete. Then she casually mentioned this cake recipe, which has been in her family forever. "Whenever I tried to make it parve, it just wasn't the same," she said. Sounds like I have a place where it belongs. Right here. —V.

Cheese Twists

INGREDIENTS

1 (1.1-lb) package puff pastry dough

CHEESE MIXTURE:

2 (8-oz) containers whipped cream cheese

½ cup sugar

1 egg yolk

1 tsp vanilla extract

NUT MIXTURE:

1 cup slivered almonds

1 cup sugar

1 tsp vanilla extract

• confectioners' sugar, for dusting

INSTRUCTIONS

1. Divide puff pastry into 2 sheets. Roll out each puff pastry sheet into a 10 x 14-inch rectangle. Refrigerate, covered, for 30 minutes.

2. Preheat oven to 350°F. Line a baking sheet with parchment paper.

3. Prepare the cheese mixture: In a medium bowl, combine cream cheese, sugar, egg yolk, and vanilla.

4. Prepare the nut mixture: In a medium bowl, combine almonds, sugar, and vanilla.

5. Spread half the cream cheese mixture over one pastry rectangle. Sprinkle with half the nut mixture. Top with the second pastry rectangle. Spread with remaining cream cheese mixture; sprinkle with remaining nut mixture.

6. Slice dough in half lengthwise (you should now have two 10 x 7-inch rectangles) and cut each section (on the narrower side) into half-inch strips. Lift up the two ends of each strip and twist. Place twists onto prepared baking sheet. Bake for 18-20 minutes, until golden. Let cool. Keep frozen until ready to serve. Dust with lots of confectioners' sugar before serving.

YIELD
30 twists

For a parve version, replace the cheese mixture with an egg white ….

WHILE I don't stock puff pastry in my freezer, this is one recipe that makes me not want to give it up. It's been passed around my family for years and it's time to publish it. If I close my eyes and imagine myself eating it, I taste the best sweet combination of dough and cheese ever, with a light creaminess and a little crispiness from the nuts.

–L.

No-Mixer Chocolate Chunk Cookies

INGREDIENTS

1 cup	brown sugar
½ cup	sugar
½ cup	oil
½ cup	(1 stick) butter, melted
2	eggs
1 tsp	vanilla extract
2½ cups	flour
1 tsp	baking soda
½ tsp	kosher salt
1 cup	chopped milk chocolate

INSTRUCTIONS

1. Preheat oven to 350°F. Line a baking sheet with parchment paper.

2. In a large bowl, combine sugars, oil, and melted butter. Use a fork to stir together. Add eggs and vanilla; mix to combine. Add flour, baking soda, and salt. Mix well. Stir in chopped chocolate.

3. Form dough into small balls (this is easier to do using a cookie scoop) and place on prepared baking sheet, about 2 inches apart. Bake for 8-10 minutes. Let cool for 5 minutes before removing from baking sheet.

YIELD
36 cookies

INSPIRED BY COOKKOSHER MEMBER
CHEF102

For a parve cookie, omit the butter and use 1 cup total oil. You'll also need bitter-sweet or semi-sweet chocolate. For more "Make It Parve" ideas, see page 126.

We love to use a praline milk chocolate bar in this recipe.

LaST minute. No time. These cookies take minutes to put together and — the best part — there's only one bowl to wash (I've even mixed these in large re-sealable plastic bags for even less cleanup, but it's still easier in a bowl). In my house, parve chocolate chunk cookies disappear quickly. Dairy chocolate chunk cookies disappear even more quickly.　　　　　−L.

Lemon Curd Ice Cream

INGREDIENTS

- 1 graham cracker pie crust
- 5 egg yolks
- • juice and zest of 4 lemons (about ⅓ cup juice)
- 1 cup sugar
- 2 cups heavy cream

INSTRUCTIONS

1. Crumble pie crust and sprinkle crumbs into the bottom of individual serving dishes (or one large serving dish). Set aside.

2. Combine egg yolks, lemon juice, zest, and sugar over a double boiler. Cook, whisking constantly, until thickened, 6-8 minutes. Let cool.

3. In the bowl of an electric mixer, beat cream until stiff. Gently fold two-thirds of the lemon curd into the cream, a little at a time. It's not a problem if there are swirls of yellow in the mixture. Pipe or spoon over crumbled crust. Drizzle with remaining lemon curd. Freeze until ready to serve.

YIELD
8-10 servings

If using graham cracker crumbs instead of a pie crust, mix them with some melted butter before adding to the dish. Crushed tea biscuits also work very well.

In the photo, we topped our ice cream with whipped cream and lemon zest.

LEAH might prefer chocolate, and I might prefer vanilla, but one thing we definitely agree on is: lemon. At every dessert taste-testing, this lemon dessert disappeared first. I suppose because it's light, refreshing, and easy to finish! Our poor guests. Eating and rating desserts ... it's a tough job.   —V.

Sundae Pops

INGREDIENTS

1 quart	vanilla ice cream
½ cup	peanut butter
½ cup	chocolate OR caramel syrup
6 Tbsp	chopped peanuts
6 Tbsp	toasted coconut
6 Tbsp	mini chocolate chips OR crushed chocolate sandwich cookies

EQUIPMENT:

12	(3-oz) paper "Dixie" cups
12	craft sticks or lollipop sticks

INSTRUCTIONS

1. Place a small scoop of ice cream into the bottom of each cup. Press down with the back of a spoon to smoothen.

2. Place peanut butter into a microwave-safe bowl and microwave for 45 seconds (this will make it easier to work with). Spoon a layer of softened peanut butter and a layer of syrup over ice cream. Top with ¼ teaspoon each peanuts, coconut, and chocolate chips.

3. Continue to layer ice cream, peanut butter, syrup, and toppings until the cup is full, pressing down the ingredients to pack them in tightly. The last layer should be ice cream.

4. Press a stick into the center of each cup. Freeze overnight.

5. To eat, tear off paper cup immediately after removing from freezer.

YIELD

12 pops

TIDBIT:

The source of the word "sundae" is unclear. One possible origin is the German word Sünde, meaning sin, alluding to the calorie-rich nature of a Sundae.

THIS is one of those treats that you prepare for the kids... but the adults end up grabbing them too. My children even love helping me add the ingredients and ice cream to the cups (they also help make a big mess). —V.

Strawberry Cheesecake Ice Cream

INGREDIENTS

CHEESECAKE CHUNKS:

1	(8-oz) container cream cheese
1	egg
¼ cup	sugar
½ tsp	vanilla extract
1	graham cracker pie crust

ICE CREAM:

1	(8-oz) container cream cheese
¾ cup	sugar
3	egg yolks
1 cup	heavy cream
8 oz	(½ bag) frozen strawberries, completely thawed

INSTRUCTIONS

1. Prepare the cheesecake chunks: Preheat oven to 350°F. In the bowl of an electric mixer, combine cream cheese, egg, sugar, and vanilla. Pour into pie crust. The filling won't fill the entire crust. Bake for 25 minutes or until top is springy to the touch. Let cool; freeze.

2. While cheesecake is baking, prepare ice cream: In the bowl of an electric mixer, combine cream cheese, sugar, and egg yolks. Whip until smooth. Remove from bowl; set aside.

3. In the bowl of an electric mixer, beat heavy cream until stiff.

4. Use a blender or immersion blender, process strawberries until smooth (you should have 1 cup strawberry purée). Add to whipped cream and stir to combine. Fold in cream cheese mixture.

5. Pour ice cream into individual serving dishes or one large serving dish. Freeze until slightly set, about 30 minutes.

6. Remove cheesecake from freezer, turn upside down, and cut into small squares. Top ice cream with cheesecake chunks and keep frozen until ready to serve.

YIELD
8 servings

Egg yolks add creaminess to no-mixer ice cream recipes, but if you want to cook your egg yolks, combine yolks and 3 tablespoons cream over a double boiler. Whisk occasionally until yolks reach 160°F, about 8 minutes. The liquid yolks will now be cooked, eliminating the risk of salmonella.

Double the recipe if you want to make a large, pretty ice cream cake in a springform pan.

I first prepared this dessert in the summertime, and I made it over and over that year. During the winter, I moved on to try new recipes. After a few months without strawberry cheesecake ice cream, though, my family complained. Now, it's on the winter menu too. (We also enjoy the parve version after meat meals.)   —V.

Make It Parve

SOURCES:

SET YOUR TABLE. Lakewood, NJ and Monsey, NY. 732.987.5569. Dishes, cutlery, and glasses as featured on pages 20, 34, 40, 44, 51, 59, 63, 93, 113, and 125

THE TABLE by Chaya Sarah Thau 732.779.4429 Tablecloths on pages 33, 55, and 61

CB2. *www.cb2.com.* Dishes and tray as featured on pages 29, 33, 49, 121

CONTAINER AND PACKAGING *www.containerandpackaging.com* Bottles, page 23

CRATE AND BARREL. *www.crateandbarrel.com* Ramekins, page 111

IKEA. *www.ikea.com.* Dishes and glasses as featured on pages 36, 55, 57, 97, 119, 121

NORPRO. *www.norpro.com* Mini cheesecake pan with removable bottoms, page 101

PACK N'WOOD. *www.packnwood.com* Wooden crate, page 101

Remaining props and backgrounds, **AMIT FARBER** and **RENEE MULLER COLLECTIONS**

MANY THANKS TO

DEC -- 2019